CULTURAL INFLUENCES
ON RESEARCH METHODS
AND STATISTICS

CULTURAL INFLUENCES ON RESEARCH METHODS AND STATISTICS

WAVELAND

PRESS, INC.

Long Grove, Illinois

For information about this book, contact:
Waveland Press, Inc.
4180 IL Route 83, Suite 101
Long Grove, IL 60047-9580
(847) 634-0081
info@waveland.com
www.waveland.com

10-digit ISBN 1-57766-112-5
13-digit ISBN 978-1-57766-112-2

Printed in the United States of America

9   8   7   6   5   4

ᴑ

Dedication

This book is dedicated to all the current and former volunteer staff members of the Intercultural and Emotion Research Laboratory. Their hard work and dedication through the years have enabled our cross-cultural research program to blossom into what it is today. I hope that our work together has touched their lives just as much as they have touched mine.

Manish Assar	Michael Biehl
Bonny Brown	Deborah Chalmers
Jaclyn Chan	Lisa Chan
Smita Chand	Andrea Chang
Kristina Duenas	Debora Fletcher
Kristin Gismervik	Martine Ham
Valerie Hearn	William Irwin
Fazilet Kasri	Helena Kenrick
Masami Kobayashi	Mary Killeen
Deborah Krupp	Cenita Kupperbusch
Mija Lee	Minjoo Lee
Nicole Lozier	Galin Luk
Erika Maniatis	Scott Matsubayashi
Loren McCarter	Patricia McKinney
Eli Medina	Erin Milligan
Erin Nishimura	Ken Preston
Bill Roberts	Judith Roberts
Liz Schloss	Adrienne Short
Donna Solomon	Beth Tafe
Sachiko Takeuchi	Jarrett Tom
Veronica Ton	Michiko Tomioka
Gia Truong	Michelle Weissman
Nathan Yrizarry	

᳄᳄

About the Author

David Matsumoto (Ph.D., University of California, Berkeley) is an Associate Professor of Psychology and Director of the Intercultural and Emotion Research Laboratory at San Francisco State University. He is the author of more than 70 works on culture and emotion, including original research articles, papers, books, book chapters, videotapes, and assessment instruments. He has addressed professional and scientific groups in the United States and internationally, including the Russian Academy of Sciences. His book, *People: Psychology from a Cultural Perspective* (also available from Waveland Press), addresses cross-cultural issues in introductory psychology.

∽

Preface

The Purpose of This Book

One of the hottest issues on American campuses today is cultural diversity. Universities across the nation are racing to develop ways by which they can incorporate teaching and learning about cultural diversity into the curricula. Faculty and students alike come from increasingly different and diverse cultural backgrounds; they are clamoring for such development. Many local, state, federal, and private regulatory agencies mandate such training for professional accreditation. Indeed, cultural diversity training in institutions of higher education is a must in our increasingly diverse world.

Psychology as a discipline is one of the leaders in the development of sensitivity to and awareness of issues of cultural diversity. Many books, videotapes, and other resources are available to help psychologists teach a variety of areas of psychology with a multicultural slant. The infusion of culture in psychology starts at the introductory level, but it also pervades courses in personality, psychopathology and clinical psychology, developmental psychology, perception and cognition, and social psychology. In each of these areas, we can find ways of incorporating issues pertaining to cultural diversity to add to, complement, and challenge the material traditionally covered in these courses.

Despite these developments, many people believe that courses on research methods and statistics are relatively insulated from issues of cultural diversity. Indeed, these types of courses seems to be where the infusion of issues of cultural diversity has been the slowest. There are probably many reasons to explain this, not the least of which has been the speed (or lack thereof) of our own recognition that cultural diversity can and does play a large role in the conduct of psychological research. Also, even among those who have felt that such issues are important, there are often insufficient resources by which we could learn more about them and impart them to our students.

This book addresses that void. It summarizes many of the key issues that concern cultural diversity in relation to methodology and statistics in research. It gives students and faculty alike some tools with which they can critically evaluate cross-cultural research better than they can with the traditional textbook pointers on methods and statistics. It gives students tips on how to conduct their own cross-cultural research. It provides a more detailed bibliography for further reading and study on these issues. Finally, it provides background material about cross-cultural psychology and research in general.

Who This Book Is For

This book is intended for use in undergraduate research methods and statistics courses in psychology or sociology, at either the upper or lower level. It can also be used as a supplement in cross-cultural psychology courses at the undergraduate or graduate level. In some cases, it may also be used as a brief review of these issues in graduate-level methods and statistics courses.

The book is written at an introductory, undergraduate level, in language that is relatively easy to follow. The straightforward examples demonstrate how cultural differences in response tendencies can be teased out of a data set.

This book is meant to supplement textbooks and other resources on research methods and statistics that are already available. It is not meant to be used as a substitute for training in traditional methodology and data analysis. Instead, it is a general yet scholarly introduction to these issues, in most cases to be used after students have had some exposure to issues of sampling, measurement, and elementary data analysis.

This book, to my knowledge, is the only resource that is available on these issues that is written for a general, undergraduate audience.

How This Book Works

The book is divided into six chapters and a reference section:

- Chapter 1 is a brief primer on cross-cultural psychology and research.
- Chapter 2 provides a brief introduction to the importance of research methods and statistics and the process of doing research.
- Chapter 3 describes in detail how cultures can influence decisions concerning research methodology, including sampling, measurement, and procedures.
- Chapter 4 describes a variety of statistical techniques that can be used to deal with cultural differences in response sets, as well as cultural influences on the interpretation of data from cross-cultural studies.
- Chapter 5 provides students with tips on how to conduct their own cross-cultural studies.
- Chapter 6 offers a conclusion to the book.
- The last section, References and Resources, is a bibliographical listing of a variety of resources on culture in general and on cross-cultural research methods in specific. These resources are much more advanced, written mostly for researchers who are serious about continuing their study of cross-cultural research methods.

Most courses, instructors, and main textbooks provide information that overlaps one or more of these areas. This means that the information in one or more of these chapters is probably redundant with something you are already studying. To help you identify those areas in this book that are *not* already covered in your course—and thus eliminate the redundancy—read the section entitled A Message to Teachers and Students: How Best to Use This Book, beginning on page xv.

You will find that using this book in your course does much more justice to the issues of cultural diversity than simply adding example boxes or small sections to existing textbooks. Yet it is a manageable addition to your students' reading list in a one- or two-semester course on methods and statistics. This approach also gives you the power to choose which chapters of this book are most appropriate for your class.

Acknowledgments

Like many of you, I have taught research methodology and statistics all my professional academic life. I believe that courses in
methods and statistics, whether on the undergraduate or graduate level, are some of the most important courses in a student's
academic career. These courses not only teach about research
in psychology, they also teach students how to be critical think-
ers about psychology, research, and life in general. Methods and
statistics instructors are truly some of the unsung heroes of
teaching psychology. Before I acknowledge the people who had
something to do with this specific book, my hat goes off to all
of you, for your work every day in the classroom, laboratory,
and field.

The idea for this book came out of a brainstorming session
that included Marianne Taflinger, Pat Gadban, and Vicki Knight.
I am grateful to all of them for encouraging me to pursue this
idea, in addition to all our other collaborative projects on cultural
diversity in psychology.

I am indebted to my editor, Jim Brace-Thompson, for his
patience and encouragement during this project, from inception
to completion. I am also indebted to Cat Collins, who made sure
paperwork and messages between us were conveyed in a timely
and professional manner. I extend my gratitude to Roxane Buck
Ezcurra, Susan Haberkorn, and Laurie Jackson for their contributions to this project.

A number of readers and reviewers provided helpful com-
ments and suggestions to our original proposal and to the final
draft: Linda Allred, East Carolina University; Bryan C. Auday,
Gordon College; Bernard Beins, Ithaca College; Dorothee
Dietrich, Hamline University; Ebrahim Fakouri, Indiana State
University; Tom Gilovich, Cornell University; Leon Ginsberg,
University of South Carolina; Mary Kite, Ball State University;
David Kreiner, Central Missouri State University; Brian Schrader,
St. Xavier University; and Shuqiang Zhang, University of Hawaii
at Manoa. Their enthusiasm for this project was perhaps more
encouragement to complete the project than any other factors
involved.

A special thanks goes to all who have taught me about
research methods and statistics in my career: Paul Ekman, Wally
Friesen, Sheldon Korchin, Phil Cowan, Bill Meredith, Bill

Saufley, Geoff Keppel, and Sheldon Zedeck. In addition, appreciation goes to all the countless, anonymous reviewers and journal editors of our research manuscripts over the years who have sharpened and improved the process of cross-cultural research. My research laboratory, the Intercultural and Emotion Research Laboratory, is based at San Francisco State University. Here I enjoy the company and hard work of a dedicated staff of assistants who engage in the process of research in exchange for little more than the joy of learning and productivity. I am extremely indebted to those in my laboratory now and over the last ten years. I am especially indebted to Michelle Weissman and Michiko Tomioka, who provided me with valuable comments and suggestions on an earlier draft of this book as well as material for the statistical examples. Both of them have become accomplished cross-cultural researchers in their own right. I am also indebted to Erin Milligan and the members of her research and development team in my laboratory who worked on the bibliography (Sachiko Takeuchi, Nicole Lozier, Jaclyn Chan, and Nathan Yrizarry). All my staff's work and friendship over the years have made this project a reality.

My friends and family have supported my work over the years. There is little I can do to repay them for their patience and understanding, support and encouragement to produce resources such as this one.

Thanks to all of you who made this happen.

David Matsumoto

ᵕᏫᐧ

A Message to Teachers
and Students:
How Best to Use This Book

Culture in Research Methods and Statistics?

You may be wondering why on earth you are about to learn
about how culture influences research methods and statistics in
psychology. If you have doubts about how and why culture
should be taught in your methods and statistics courses, you are
definitely not alone.

Issues of culture and diversity are very fashionable now
on university and college campuses across America. Many psychology departments are struggling to find ways to infuse their
curricula with resources on culture and with faculty who are
knowledgeable about diversity and who can meet the chal-
lenges of our changing world. In psychology, most of our ef-
forts have involved the addition of courses on cultural diversity
and cross-cultural psychology. Also, many psychology departments and faculties are incorporating issues of culture and diversity in other, mainstream psychology courses. Thus, it is not
uncommon today to learn about cross-cultural issues in introductory psychology, development, clinical, abnormal, and social psychology.

Still, courses on research methods and statistics have traditionally been insulated against this onslaught of innovations. Indeed, many faculty and students alike have felt that culture does
not affect the conduct of research or data analysis. Few people
give second thought to the possibility that culture may influence
research. Consequently, issues of cultural diversity are not typically covered in courses on methods and statistics.

The goal of this book is to let you know that culture can, and does, have dramatic effects on the ways in which we conduct research and analyze data in psychology. Here we will describe many of those ways to you, so that you can better understand exactly how, and why, these effects occur. If you read closely, you will probably see that many of the issues described in this book are actually extensions of general issues in research methodology and statistics. The only unique thing about them is that they are manifestations of those issues with regard to *cultural* influences. In addition, you will find issues that are truly unique to research across cultures, such as problems related to translation.

As you read and learn more about cultural influences in methodology and statistics, you will also notice that many of these issues are applicable not only to the conduct of research in different countries and nations, but also to research comparing people of different ethnicities and races, both within and across countries, as well as across gender. We hope that you apply many of the cross-cultural issues that you learn here to these other types of research as well.

The Structure of This Book and How Best to Use It

As described in the preface, this book is divided into six chapters and a section on references and resources, each with a different purpose and audience. *It is important for you to choose which sections are most germane to your class.*

- Chapter 1 is a brief primer on cross-cultural psychology and research. *This material is intended for students who have had no training in cross-cultural research or psychology.*
- Chapter 2 provides a brief introduction to the importance of research methods and statistics and the process of doing research. *This material is intended for students who have had no training in research methods.*
- Chapter 3 describes in detail how culture can influence decisions concerning research methodology, including sampling, measurement, and procedures. *This material is intended for students who have training in research meth-*

ods and want to extend their training into cross-cultural research.

- Chapter 4 describes a variety of statistical techniques that can be used to deal with cultural differences in response sets, as well as cultural influences on the interpretation of data from cross-cultural studies. *This material is intended for students who have had training in statistics, particularly one- and two-factor analysis of variance and chi-square.*
- Chapter 5 provides students with tips on how to conduct their own cross-cultural studies. *This material is intended for students who will be conducting their own project.*
- Chapter 6 offers a conclusion to the book, *appropriate for all readers.*
- The last section, References and Resources, is a bibliographical listing of a variety of resources on culture in general and on cross-cultural research methods in particular. *This material is intended for students who want to do more reading on cross-cultural psychology or research methods.*

Most courses, instructors, and main textbooks provide information that overlaps one or more of these areas. This means that the information in one or more of these chapters is probably redundant with something you are already studying in class. You need to identify those areas in this book that are pertinent for your course or interests and assign those sections for reading. *If you or your students have already covered the material of any section, skip it.* This will eliminate redundancy.

Still, this book can stand on its own, taken as a collective whole. The structure of this book lets you use any part or all of this book as you deem most appropriate. Every class and instructor will have a different approach, and we hope that this book provides sufficient flexibility while covering the important issues.

ᴑ

Contents

1

⌒

A Brief Introduction to
Cross-Cultural Psychology
and Research

What Are Cross-Cultural Psychology
and Cross-Cultural Research?

Learning about cross-cultural psychology in general may not appear *directly* related to cultural influences on research. But it is an important first step in understanding cultural influences on the research process. You need to have some background in cross-cultural psychology as a general field. With that background, you will be in a better position to understand cross-cultural research and cultural influences on methodology and statistics.

To learn more about cross-cultural psychology in general, let's first take a look at how we in psychology come to know what is "truth" about people.

The Nature of Truth in Psychology:
The Importance of Research

Psychologists interested in generating knowledge about people generally rely on a single type of process to generate that knowledge. That process is known as *research*. There are many different types of research, and all psychologists interested in generating knowledge about people rely on some type of research.

Research is the primary way by which psychologists uncover "truths" about the world. Indeed, that's the reason you *need* to take this course on methodology and/or statistics! Almost all academic fields related to human behavior rely heavily on scientific research to generate what knowledge we have about how and why people behave. Before we accept something as a "truth," we have to be assured that the research that produced that truth met some minimal standards for scientific rigor. Thus, the truth that was borne from the research could be only that and nothing else.

Truth is never generated from a single study. No matter how well any one study was conducted, most scientists and scholars will not accept its results as a general truth, and for good reason. Every study is conducted under certain conditions, or research parameters. These conditions form the basis for the limitations to the knowledge that is generated in that study. Whatever result was obtained from any single study, therefore, is bounded by those conditions and parameters and, thus, limitations.

For a finding to be considered a truth through the research process, it is important that virtually the same study be conducted again, with different participants under different parameters and conditions. If researchers obtain virtually the same finding, despite having changed a number of parameters of the research, then we can say that the findings have been repeated over a number of different studies. Sometimes these studies are conducted by the same researcher or research team, sometimes not. In either case, when virtually the same result is obtained, we call this repeated finding a *replication*. When a finding is replicated, psychologists start to believe that the finding says something true about human behavior. Thus, replicated findings form the basis for "truths" in psychology.

Truth and knowledge, therefore, are dependent on how the research that produced those truths was conducted.

In addition to the scientists who actually do research, many scholars are active consumers of research. These scholars digest completed research and translate the findings for use by others (such as students like you). Research, therefore, plays a major role not only in generating knowledge and testing ideas, but also in communicating that knowledge to others.

What Are Cross-Cultural Psychology and Research, and How Do They Affect Psychological Truths?

Cross-cultural psychology is a branch of psychology that is primarily concerned with testing possible limitations to knowledge by studying people of different cultures. In its strictest sense, cross-cultural research involves simply including participants from different cultural backgrounds and testing possible differences among them. In its broadest sense, however, cross-cultural psychology is concerned with understanding truth and psychological principles as either universal (that is, true for all people of all cultures) or culture-specific (true for some people of some cultures).

Cross-cultural psychology is not topic-specific. That is, cross-cultural psychologists are interested in a broad range of phenomena related to human behavior, from perception to language, child-rearing to psychopathology. What delineates cross-cultural psychology from "traditional" or "mainstream" psychology, therefore, is not the phenomenon of interest. Rather, it is the commonality in testing limitations to knowledge by examining whether that knowledge is applicable to or obtainable in people of different cultural backgrounds. Given this definition, cross-cultural psychologists can apply cross-cultural techniques in testing the universality or cultural specificity of any and all aspects of human behavior. In this fashion, cross-cultural psychology and research can offer alternatives to what is typically presented as psychological "truth" that is borne from studies within a single culture.

Before proceeding much further, however, we need to deal with what is meant by the word *culture*. If we are going to learn more about cultural influences on the research process, then we should learn exactly what culture is.

A Definition of Culture

Despite the fact that most of us probably feel that we know what culture is, culture is a rather difficult concept to define formally. When asked, many people typically think that culture is race or ethnicity and equate culture with rituals, customs, food, and music.

Certainly, there are many aspects to culture, such as music, food, religion, child-rearing patterns, ways of thinking, and the like. It is also certain that no single aspect can adequately capture all of what culture is. For our purposes in learning about cultural influences on research and data analysis, however, we need to adopt *some* approach to understanding culture and *some* kind of definition.

Fortunately, many scholars in anthropology and sociology as well as psychology have offered a number of interesting definitions of culture that we can use to better understand cultural influences on research. For our purposes, we define culture as *the set of attitudes, values, beliefs, and behaviors, shared by a group of people, communicated from one generation to the next via language or some other means of communication* (Barnouw, 1985).

This definition of culture is "fuzzy." That is, there are necessarily no hard and fast rules of how to determine what a culture is or who belongs to that culture. In this sense, culture is a sociopsychological construct, a sharing across people of psychological phenomena such as values, attitudes, beliefs, and behaviors. Members of the same culture share these psychological phenomena. Members of different cultures do not.

Culture is not necessarily rooted in physical characteristics. That is, culture is not race. Two people of the same race can either share the same values and behaviors—that is, culture—or they can be very disparate in their cultural makeups. Now, it is true that people of the same racial heritage may in general share the same socialization processes and may be enculturated in similar ways. Thus, we may speak of a Hispanic culture or an African American culture or an Asian culture. But it is also true that there need not be a one-to-one correspondence between race and culture. Just because one is born a certain race does not necessarily mean that one adopts the culture that is stereotypic of that race.

Culture is also not nationality. Just because a person is from France, for example, does not necessarily mean that he or she will act in accordance with what one would consider the dominant French culture or with our stereotypes of French people. Just as culture does not necessarily conform to race or racial stereotypes, culture also does not necessarily conform to nationality or citizenship. In fact, there is ample and growing evidence to suggest that a small but substantial portion of the population of many different countries do not "match" the dominant cultural stereotype of their country (Triandis, 1992).

In this sense, culture is as much an individual, psychological construct as it is a macro, social construct. That is, to some extent, culture exists in each and every one of us individually as much as it exists as a global, social construct. Individual differences in culture can be observed among people in the degree to which they adopt and engage in the attitudes, values, beliefs, and behaviors that, by consensus, constitute their culture. If you act in accordance with those shared values or behaviors, then that culture resides in you; if you do not share those values or behaviors, then you do not share that culture.

Emics, Etics, Ethnocentrism, and Stereotypes

One of the major ways of conceptualizing principles in cross-cultural psychology is through the use of the terms *emics* and *etics*. These terms are related to the universality or cultural specificity of knowledge and truths. An etic refers to findings that appear to be consistent across different cultures; that is, an etic refers to a universal truth or principle. An emic, in contrast, refers to findings that appear to be different across cultures; an emic, therefore, refers to truths that are culture-specific.

The concepts of emics and etics are powerful because of the implications to what we may know as truth. If we know something about human behavior and we regard it as a truth, *and* it is an etic (that is, universal), then the truth as we know it is truth for all, regardless of culture. If our knowledge about human behavior, however, is an emic (that is, culture-specific), then that "truth" is not necessarily true for someone of another culture. Truth, in this sense, is relative, not absolute. This definition of truth with regard to emics and etics should force us all to consider what we believe is true or not.

There are many examples of both emics and etics in psychology. Indeed, one of the major goals of cross-cultural psychology as a discipline is to uncover exactly which aspects of human behavior are emics and which are etics.

In general, most cross-cultural psychologists would agree that there are just as many, if not more, emics as there are etics. That is, people of different cultures actually do find ways to differ with respect to most aspects of human behavior. In a sense, that is not surprising. Each culture evolves in its own distinct way to "manage" human behaviors in the most efficient and appropriate fashion to ensure survival. These ways differ depending on population density, availability of food and other resources, and the like. To the extent that each culture must meet different needs in the environment, each culture will develop differences in the ways in which it impacts on the people within it.

The existence of many emics, or cultural differences, is not problematic in and of itself. There is potential for problem, however, when one attempts to interpret the reasons underlying or producing those differences. Because we all exist in our own cultures with our own cultural backgrounds, we tend to see things through that background. That is, culture acts as a filter, not only when we perceive things, but also when we think about and interpret events. We may interpret another person's behavior from our own cultural background and make some conclusion about that behavior on the basis of our own beliefs of culture and behavior. Our interpretation may be wrong, however, if the behavior that we are judging originates from a different cultural orientation than our own. In some cases (more than we all think!), we may be way off in our interpretation of other people's behavior.

For example, suppose you are having a conversation with a person from a different culture. While you are talking with this person, you notice that she does not really make eye contact with you when she speaks. Also, she does not look at you when you speak. On the few occasions when she looks your way, she quickly averts her gaze if your eyes meet. From your cultural background, you may interpret that she does not feel very positive about you or your interaction. You may even begin to feel put off and reject any attempts at future interaction. You may not feel trusting or close to her. However, she may come from a culture in which direct gazing is discouraged or is even a sign of arrogance or a slight. She may actually be avoiding eye contact not because of any negative feelings, but out of deference and politeness. Of course, these potential problems have real and practical implications in everyday life. Think about this scenario occurring in a job interview, in a teaching/learning situation, during a business negotiation, or even in a visit with your therapist!

Still, sometimes we cannot separate ourselves from our own cultural backgrounds and biases to understand the behaviors of others. This type of resistance forms the basis of what is known as *ethnocentrism*—the interpretation of others' behavior through one's own cultural glasses. All people—students and faculty, laypersons and researchers—need to be aware of these biases and tendencies in understanding the behaviors of others of different cultural backgrounds.

Ethnocentrism is closely related to two other important topics—stereotypes and images. *Images* are representations that we all hold about our expectations of others' behaviors. Images can be positive, negative, or neutral. When those images of people from a different culture are negative, we often call those negative images stereotypes. *Stereotypes* are fixed attitudes, beliefs, or opinions about people who belong to cultures other than one's own. They may be born of fact. Often, however, stereotypes are combinations of fact and fiction about people from a certain cultural group. Images can give people some kind of basis for judging, evaluating, and interacting with people of other cultures. But stereotypes can be dangerous and damaging when people adhere to them inflexibly and apply them to all people of that cultural background without recognizing the possible false bases of the stereotype as well as individual differences within that culture.

We often find, either through formal research or through our everyday experiences, that we are different from people of other cultures. Our discovery of these differences can have serious negative consequences when values such as good/bad, right/wrong, superior/inferior are attached to the behaviors of others. For example, consider a hypothetical scenario where researchers report that they have found differences in IQ (intelligence quotient) test scores between African American and European American participants. In and of itself this is still "just" a finding. However, some people may interpret this finding as "proof" that European Americans are genetically or biologically smarter than African Americans. This would cause quite a stir and may even prevent people from engaging in a constructive search for other interpretations (for example, the cultural bias that may be inherent in the testing procedures).

Emics, etics, ethnocentrism, and stereotypes are all important concepts to learn about and remember. As we progress through our studies of cultural similarities and differences, it is important to have some idea of the potential pitfalls. Needless to say, making value statements, maintaining an ethnocentric attitude, and adhering inflexibly to stereotypes are not conducive to progress in this field.

Incorporating Cross-Cultural Issues in Learning about Psychology

There is a *lot* of information in the field of psychology that American psychologists and students consider to be truth. The comprehensiveness of most psychology textbooks and the density of most course syllabi attest to the fact that there is a lot of stuff out there to be learned.

Still, it is vitally important now to incorporate cross-cultural issues into our knowledge and learning base of psychology for at least two reasons. The first has to do with what we call "scientific philosophy." The name may look scary, but scientific philosophy simply refers to what we have been discussing all along in this book—the need to evaluate our truths in terms of the parameters under which those truths were obtained. More simply put, we need to examine whether the information we have learned (or will learn in the future) is applicable to *all* people of *all* cultures (that is, it is an etic) or only to *some* people of *some* cultures (in which case, it is an emic). Scientific philosophy refers to the notion that we have a duty, an obligation, to ask these questions about the scientific process and about the nature of the truths we have learned, or will learn, in psychology.

The second reason that it is important to incorporate cross-cultural issues in psychology is much more practical. Psychology involves the study of human behavior to improve our understanding of people. One of the goals of this endeavor is to help us in our real-life, everyday interactions with others. As we have more frequent contact with people of different cultural backgrounds, it becomes increasingly imperative that we learn about emics and etics in our truths and beliefs about people. To be ignorant of such emics and etics would make us guilty of ethnocentrism and would hamper our everyday dealings with others.

Incorporating cross-cultural issues in mainstream psychology means that we need to ask some very basic, yet extremely important, questions about the nature of the truths taught in psychology classes across America today. Those questions are addressed by cross-cultural psychology and research.

Understanding Cross-Cultural Research

The primary importance of cross-cultural research lies in its test of the limitations and boundaries to the knowledge generated from research in only a single culture or country. Through cross-cultural research, we can gain a better understanding of what aspects of human behavior are universal—that is, pancultural, or applicable to all people—and what aspects are culture-specific—that is, true for only some people. Ultimately, we can gain a better appreciation of the breadth and scope of human behavior.

Thus, it is important to learn more about cross-cultural research, just as it is important to learn about research methodology and statistics in general. In fact, it is vital to learn about these influences if one is to be a critical consumer of cross-cultural research or an able cross-cultural researcher.

2

∽

A Brief Discussion of
Issues Related to
Research Methods and Statistics

The Parameters and Conditions of Research

To be active, informed, and critical consumers of research, we must gain some basic understanding of research methodology. Only with a good understanding can we evaluate the research on its own merits and decide whether or not to believe a research report. If a study employed what you think are faulty procedures, then you will not (and should not) believe the results of that study, no matter how attractive (or politically correct) those results appear. In contrast, if the procedures appear to be problem-free and the data generated by those procedures seem believable, then you would be likely to decide that the results are true.

To make informed and critical decisions, we need to have some working understanding of research methods, beginning with the general parameters and conditions under which most studies are conducted.

All studies on human behavior are conducted under some conditions, with certain parameters and certain limitations. These conditions exist because it is impossible to study *all* people on *all* behaviors under *all* parameters and conditions. So, researchers need to make many decisions when conducting a study. Each decision forms the basis for the conditions, parameters, and, thus, limitations to a study. All knowledge generated by research is bounded by these parameters and limitations.

Many researchers are not aware of how many decisions they make in conducting a study. The reason for this is that many of the decisions are made automatically or by default, be- cause "it is the way things are generally done" or because "an- other study did it this way." As researchers gain experience in conducting research, and especially in thinking about how to conduct research, they become more keenly aware of the many decisions made in conducting a study.

What are some of these decisions? In the rest of this chap- ter we will outline just several of the major types of decisions made in a study. When conducting a specific study, a researcher will actually make many more specific decisions.

The Nature of the Question Being Asked: The Choice of Hypothesis

One of the first decisions researchers make in conducting a study concerns what question they want to address or what hy- pothesis they want to test. Every study attempts to answer a par- ticular question. For example, a researcher may want to find out whether boys or girls in elementary school do better at a par- ticular type of problem, or whether the number of people in a given area is related to certain types of health problems.

In the typical course of research, the researchers develop a question to ask and then design a study to answer it. Con- versely, every study, by default, answers some question. Even if you do not know what question a researcher is trying to an- swer, you should be able to surmise what that question is just by reading about the study. Sometimes the question that the researcher starts with is not addressed by the study he or she conducts!

In any case, determining just what question to ask is the first decision a researcher makes.

The Type of Research Paradigm Chosen to Address the Question

Once researchers decide what question to address, they need to select a general research approach, or paradigm, to answer it. There are many different types of general approaches that re- searchers can use—for example, the case study, longitudinal re- search, experimental research, correlational research, quasi-experimental research, and the like. Public health research may use an epidemiological approach to understanding the causes of different types of health outcomes and diseases. Sociological research may use social markers and other institutions to delineate social change and its impact on people. Anthropological research may use in-depth studies of single cultures, where researchers immerse themselves in a culture and try to learn everything about it. Research in economics and business may study the number and types of industries or look at changes in gross domestic products or other economic indicators.

To address the chosen question, the researcher needs to choose one of the many approaches available. The general approach is often linked to the question, so that a researcher may not give much thought to choosing an approach, assuming that the approach appropriate to the question is a "given."

Nevertheless, the approach that is used to conduct the actual study is a decision made by the researcher, by default or not. This decision, in turn, further defines and places conditions, restrictions, and limitations on the study and the information generated from it.

The Nature of the Participants in the Study

The basic "unit" included in a study—also referred to as the "unit of analysis"—is what is used to gather the primary information. In most studies on human behavior in psychology, for example, the "unit" is a person (commonly referred to as a subject or participant).

Different research approaches utilize different units of analysis. As just mentioned, the most common unit of analysis in the study of human behavior, at least in psychology, is a person. Epidemiological surveys across countries may use country as the unit of analysis. Industry may be the unit of analysis in a study of the effects of different types of companies on the national economy.

Researchers decide what the exact unit of analysis is in their studies. This decision places a condition on the nature of the information, or data, generated in the study.

In addition, researchers decide how to limit the units of analysis in a study to a manageable and realistic quantity. The final group of units that is included in a study is commonly referred to as the sample. In fact, most studies require that several decisions, not one, be made to achieve a workable sample.

For example, in studies with people, researchers may decide to limit their samples to university students in the United States because students are so readily available. However, a researcher cannot possibly survey all university students in the United States in a study. Thus, the decision often made by psychology researchers is to study university students enrolled in introductory psychology courses in a single university, because these students are *the* most readily available (that is, participation in the research can be part of the course). Even then, only a small number of the students enrolled in the course at one particular time will participate. Thus, what was envisioned as a hypothesis that would be applicable to many people is actually tested with only a small, specially chosen sample of a limited nature. These choices place conditions and limitations on the nature of the information or data obtained in the study.

Conceptual and Empirical Definitions of Variables: Operationalization

In addition to decisions about samples, researchers make decisions about how to measure the variables they are interested in. How researchers measure something is closely related to how they *conceptually* define it. The way a researcher conceptually defines something dictates how it should be measured or operationalized. The method of measurement, in turn, places a limitation on the nature of the information obtained. Conversely, every method of measurement defines the nature of what is being measured *by default*. That is, even if you don't know how a researcher may conceptually define something, you should be able to guess at how he or she conceptually views it by knowing how it is measured.

For example, suppose that you are interested in studying intelligence. You need to have a conceptual definition of intelligence. Most American psychologists studying intelligence in the past believed that intelligence consists mainly of cognitive skills related to verbal and analytic abilities. Thus, instruments such as the Wechsler Adult Intelligence Scale (WAIS) were used to measure intelligence. The WAIS has 11 different types of tests, of which some are verbal and some are analytic. The verbal tests include such tests as a vocabulary test and a reading comprehension test. The analytic tests involve such tests as a jigsaw-puzzle type of picture completion and a picture arrangement test in which the subject arranges a set of pictures so that they tell a story.

In more recent studies, researchers interested in intelligence have broadened their conceptual definition of intelligence to include such things as musical, artistic, and other creative abilities, or physical, sports-type abilities. These changes, in turn, dictate changes in the ways in which these aspects of intelligence are measured.

In your study of intelligence you would need to decide how you define intelligence and then choose the method that matches your definition. The specific tasks, questionnaires, instruments, or whatever used to measure it (such as the WAIS) place conditions, and thus limitations, on the nature of the information gathered and the nature of the data generated in the study.

Environment and Setting

All research occurs somewhere, which is a further condition of the parameters of the research. Many studies in anthropology, for example, are done in the field, where the researchers visit and often live with the people and the culture that they are studying. This type of in-depth immersion in a culture dictates that the research setting or environment be the actual environment in which the people being studied live. This defines the setting under which the data, based on observation or interview, are gathered.

Many studies occur in laboratory settings. Participants are recruited (through a call for volunteers, sign-ups in a "subject pool," or the like), and they come to a designated experiment or laboratory room. There, the subjects are often met by an experimenter, who explains the purpose and procedures of the experiment. The participants may view a movie screen, interact with a computer, or do a task. In any case, this setting defines the environmental parameters within which the data will be obtained.

Many studies of human behavior are observational in nature. That is, they involve experimenters recording their observations of certain types of behaviors in a particular setting. The setting may be the university student center, a home, a village, a shopping mall—just about anywhere. *Wherever* the research takes place, that setting describes an environmental condition under which the data are collected. This condition, in turn, defines a parameter, or limitation, of the study.

Procedures

Not only do researchers need to decide the nature and measurement of the variables, the samples to be included, and the setting of the research, they also need to make more "mundane" decisions—such as which type of instructions to give to the participants, what time of day to conduct the experiment, where to find historical or archival data, and so forth. All these characteristics and activities further define the conditions of the study.

Many of these aspects of research are given little consideration by some researchers, and even less by many consumers of the research. Nevertheless, they exist and by default define the conditions, and thus limitations, under which data are obtained and knowledge generated.

How to Deal with Data

Once researchers gather data, they have to decide what to do with those data. In most cases, the researchers need to perform some type of analysis of the data either to summarize them or to infer information about them. More often than not, the need to do something with the data obtained in research leads us to statistics.

Statistics are methods that researchers use to manipulate data in order to draw some meaning from the data. Simply counting the number of times a particular behavior occurs is a statistical manipulation (called *frequency*). Determining an average of the number of times a response is obtained is also a statistical manipulation.

In some studies, the statistical manipulations can be quite complex, involving a multiple-step process with different types of outcomes. Analysis of variance, discriminant analysis, multiple regression and correlation—these are all statistical procedures. Regardless of the name and the complexity of the statistics, the procedures all have the same purpose—to transform the data into something from which the researchers can draw some meaning.

There are many different types of statistics, and they all manipulate data differently. Thus, there are many choices in analyzing data. Researchers can split their data files, using only parts of the data. They can choose this statistic or that. The specific ways researchers choose to analyze data dictate the presentation of the data. This presentation, in turn, affects the meanings that researchers, and the consumers of that research, draw from the data. Because the choice of analysis plan and the statistics affect the nature of the presentation of the data, the ways in which data are analyzed form yet another condition, or limitation, on research.

How to Interpret the Findings

In any study—psychological, sociological, anthropological, or otherwise—researchers need to draw conclusions on the basis of their data and findings. The interpretations researchers draw from a study all depend on a number of factors, including the researchers' own backgrounds and upbringings, their particular theoretical biases, and the like.

All interpretations are made under such conditions—that is, with whatever particular viewpoint the researchers bring with them to the interpretation. Because these are conditions, they are yet another way by which limitations are placed on a study.

Summary

This chapter has highlighted some of the conditions and parameters by which studies of human behavior are conducted. The decisions occur in all types of research, regardless of the hypothesis being addressed or the specific approach to answer the question.

Although these parameters and limitations must be considered in any research, cross-cultural research on human behavior engenders special problems and issues. The information presented in this chapter can be used as a foundation from which we can look at cross-cultural research methodology, how it differs from non–cross-cultural research, and the special issues it raises.

3

↝

Cultural Influences on Research Methods

Special Issues in Cross-Cultural Research Methods

Doing research in different cultures, and comparing the results you find in one culture with those found in another, involves special issues. Just as it is important for the informed and critical reader to understand some basic issues pertaining to research in general (as briefly discussed in Chapter 2), it is also important for consumers of cross-cultural research to understand basic issues pertaining to cross-cultural research. With knowledge of these basic issues, we will be in a better position to understand and evaluate information about cross-cultural similarities and differences. We will also be able to conduct better cross-cultural studies.

Many of the special issues in cross-cultural research are really extensions of issues pertaining to research in general. Some issues in cross-cultural research, however, pertain solely to research in different cultures and countries, across different languages. In this chapter, you will get a taste of just what these issues are and how they are especially important to cross-cultural studies.

Cultural Influences on Hypothesis Generation

All researchers choose hypotheses to study. This is no different in cross-cultural work. But it is important to realize in cross-cultural research that all researchers have their own cultural upbringing and backgrounds and these backgrounds influence the hypotheses chosen. These biases exist, whether they are good or bad, right or wrong, conscious or unconscious. These biases influence the types of hypotheses we think are important and, thus, what we believe should be studied in cross-cultural research. Because the research questions we formulate originate from our own personal and cultural biases, it follows that *a hypothesis or research question that is important for us may not be as important or relevant to someone from a different cultural background.*

For example, suppose you want to conduct a study that examines cultural differences in how quickly people can solve maze-type puzzles presented on a computer. It might be interesting and relevant to conduct this study in the United States, Hong Kong, and France, and compare the results of the American, Chinese, and French participants. But this study might not be as relevant to tribe members of the Kalahari in Africa or to preliterate cultures such as those indigenous to New Guinea. If these people were asked to participate in the research, they might be afraid to go near that mechanical-looking contraption (the computer).

Suppose researchers decide to study cultural differences in problem-solving ability in the United States and among tribespeople in Africa. To do this, they present subjects in both cultures with a device that must be manipulated in some way to obtain a monetary reward. Americans might be able to approach this task and be successful in it. The tribespeople from Africa, however, might believe this task to be entirely meaningless, view the contraption with fear, and not care one bit about money! Yet if the researchers present a problem-solving task of tracking different animals through different scents and footprints, then Africans might respond very positively to the task. Imagine American subjects performing such a task!

Although these examples may seem to be quite extreme, there have been similar studies. Most studies, though, are subtler in their approach to glossing over cultural differences in the importance and meaning of the research questions.

Researchers cannot decide on their own which questions are important to study across cultures and then impose those questions on participants of other cultures. More often than not, researchers assume that their hypothesis is equally important and has the same meaning in other cultures. This is an ethno-centric way of doing research, which should be avoided by first checking the validity of one's biases.

Definitions of Culture in Cross-Cultural Research

When cross-cultural researchers decide to conduct a study, they usually decide to gather data from such places as the United States, Germany, Japan, and India. That is, they gather data from different *countries*. The data are also usually gathered in a single city within each country. So, cross-cultural research is usually not even cross-national; it is cross-city. In addition, the countries to be included are generally not determined by any theoretical framework; usually, the countries are samples of convenience—for example, where the researcher has a friend who is willing to collect data. Although different cultures undoubtedly underlie different countries and cities, researchers often make an assumption, through their research methods, that countries and cities are the same as cultures.

This is an incorrect assumption, which presents a dilemma for cross-cultural researchers. As we discussed earlier, most cross-cultural scholars agree that culture is the shared conglomeration of attitudes, values, behaviors, and beliefs, communicated from one generation to the next through language. This definition of culture is subjective, not objective; sociopsychological, not biological, genetic, or physiological. That is where the problem lies.

Despite this definition of culture, cross-cultural researchers have lacked an adequate way of measuring this "sharing" of psychological characteristics in their research. Because a way of measuring this sharing does not exist, researchers rely on "easier" aspects of people to measure—for example, race (European American, Chinese, Mexican, African American, and the like) or nationality (American, Japanese, German, Brazilian, and so on). But culture is not necessarily race or nationality.

The inability of researchers to measure culture on the sociopsychological level, in accordance with our definition of culture, has resulted in a trade-off of our ability to study real cross-cultural differences. Indeed, most of the studies conducted to date have measured culture by either race or nationality. We cannot, and should not, categorically dismiss these studies or their findings. They do provide valuable information about possible cultural differences, because cultural differences do indeed underlie countries. Such studies do tell us how there may be limitations to what we know and regard as truth as produced by research from mainstream academia. But we must recognize the discrepancy between our definition of culture and the definition of culture used in the research.

The Nature of the Participants in Cross-Cultural Research

Sampling Issues

More often than not, researchers assume that a group of people in a cross-cultural study (that is, the sample) are good representatives of that particular culture. For instance, in the simplest cross-cultural research design, researchers gather a sample of people in one culture, obtain data from them, and compare those data to other data or known values. Suppose a researcher gathered a sample of 50 Americans as part of a cross-cultural study. Are the 50 Americans adequate representatives of the American culture? If they were recruited from Beverly Hills, California, would the study be the same as it would be with 50 recruits from the Bronx? From Wichita, Kansas? If the 50 participants were all of European descent, would they be an "adequate" sample? If not, what percentage of people of different racial and ethnic backgrounds would the researcher need to be satisfied (given that it is too difficult to measure "true" culture)? If the sample required 25% to be of African descent, could any African American be recruited? What criteria would be used to decide whether the sample of 50 people were adequate representatives of the American culture? What is the definition of the "American" culture, anyway?

These types of questions are endless and are not easy to resolve. Although they pertain to any sample from any culture, they are especially germane to American samples used in cross-cultural work.

Researchers need to pay particular attention to issues of sampling in the conduct of their research. Aside from being unable most of the time to measure culture on a subjective level, cross-cultural researchers too often simply assume that the participants in their studies are adequate representatives of their culture. When differences are found, researchers assume that the differences are "cultural," because they assume that the samples are representatives of culture. Who knows? The differences obtained in a study of the United States, Japan, Brazil, and Mexico may be the same as the differences in a study of Minneapolis, Los Angeles, Miami, and Newark!

Equivalence Issues

Not only are there questions about whether samples in cross-cultural studies are adequate representatives of their cultures, there are also questions about whether the samples across the cultures are equivalent to each other. For the research to be methodologically sound, researchers need to make sure that the samples they compare are somehow equivalent. This is not easy.

Suppose, for example, that a researcher plans to compare data on a task from a sample of 50 Americans from Los Angeles to the data from 50 preliterate members of the Fore tribe in New Guinea. The Americans and the Fore come from entirely different backgrounds—different socioeconomic classes, different educational levels, different social experiences, different exposure to various forms of technology, and the like. How are we to know that any differences, if found, were due to the cultures or to these other differences? Clearly, comparing data from a sample of respondents in a major, international metropolis to the data from a sample of preliterate tribes with minimal outside contact is very difficult.

Although this example is so outrageous that the two samples are obviously not equivalent, the question remains for samples that appear to be more equivalent. Consider 50 subjects from Los Angeles, 50 from Osaka, 50 from Hong Kong, and 50 from Paris. Equivalence is still an issue, despite the fact that we are now dealing only with residents of major cities.

Equivalence issues are especially important to consider given that so much cross-cultural research, like most research in psychology, is conducted using university and college students as subjects. First, we need to realize that just attending a college or university means different things in different countries and cultures. In the United States, the system of education is relatively accessible to many young adults, although it may not seem so from time to time. Young adults in American society probably have more access to a college and university system than do the young adults of any other country. There are other countries (for example, Japan) in which a higher percentage of high school graduates go on to college. But in the United States the ability to go to a college or university is almost considered an American citizen's right.

In many countries this is simply not so. For example, in India (where, by the way, much cross-cultural research has been conducted), attending a college or university is not so much a right as it is a privilege of an upper socioeconomic class who can either afford to go or were born into such privilege. If you were to conduct a cross-cultural study involving subjects in a university in the United States and those in a country such as India, certainly you would find cultural differences underlying the samples. But differences in other subject characteristics such as class and socioeconomic status would confound those cultural differences. How could you interpret found differences? Would those differences be truly reflective of cultural differences? Or might they be due to differences in class? Would you find the same types of differences if you conducted a similar study across socioeconomic classes solely in the United States?

Second, regardless of how the students made it to college, they often come to the laboratory or experiment with quite different expectations. In the United States, researchers ask for volunteers to be subjects in a study. Those who don't want to do it, don't have to. Even after the study has begun, a subject can quit at any time with no penalty. Subjects have the right to withhold use of data obtained from them, to be assured of confidentiality, and the like. Most experimenters review with the volunteers the subject's "Bill of Rights," which explains all rights as a research participant.

Students in many other countries are not afforded such "rights." In many Asian countries, for example, subjects are not recruited; they are required by an instructor simply to participate. And they *all* must participate. There is no subject's Bill of Rights, no volunteering, no assurance of confidentiality. These students are usually not taught psychology or experimentation, so they may be more afraid and apprehensive. They are given few, if any, explicit guidelines on what is appropriate and what is not.

Lest you get the wrong impression that many researchers in these countries are free to conduct whatever hideous experiments they wish, let me say that there often are mechanisms to ensure that researchers do not take advantage of student participants. These mechanisms, however, are not written and explicit; they are unspoken and social, although generally understood well enough not to overstress student participants. In many cases, the pressures of such unwritten rules produce research in the opposite direction—that is, very innocuous, often questionnaire-based, with few negative consequences.

Subjects in different countries participate in research under quite different pretenses and expectations. In dealing with these differences, cross-cultural researchers need to establish some basis of equivalence between their samples in order to make cultural comparisons meaningful. But often equivalence is not feasible because of realistic differences on these dimensions, as well as the cultural ones, between the samples in a cross-cultural study. When differences are found, researchers often assume that they reflect cultural differences, although this may not be the case. As consumers of this research we must be aware of other plausible interpretations of the data.

Measurement and Operationalization Issues in Cross-Cultural Research

Issues of measurement in cross-cultural research are especially problematic. Often, however, they are overlooked by students of cross-cultural research methods in the quest for more exciting hypotheses to study or to test. For research—cross-cultural or otherwise—to be meaningful, the methods of measurement need to be meaningful. If researchers are not measuring what they want to measure, how can their findings be trusted?

In this section, we will discuss several issues concerning measurement, especially as it relates to cross-cultural work. Let's use as an example the typical measurement procedure in psychology experiments—the questionnaire. Of course, the issues pertain to other measurement systems in cross-cultural research as well, including behavioral responses, observational coding, and so on.

The typical questionnaire identifies a concept or construct to be measured (for example, self-esteem), has multiple items (say, 50), includes subscales derived by either theoretical or empirical work (say, 4), and has a scoring procedure. Let's see how some of these characteristics come to play in cross-cultural research.

Concept and Construct Equivalence

The most overlooked aspect of measurement concerns the meanings of the variables to be studied. We tend to forget that different cultures may assign different meanings to the variables of interest in a study. If a concept means different things to people of different cultures, then it is difficult to compare data on that concept across the different cultures.

Earlier in this book, we discussed how American researchers typically defined and measured intelligence using the WAIS. Although this may be valid for studies conducted in the United States (is it?), another culture may have a different conception of what constitutes intelligence. For example, let's say a culture considers nobility of character and sincerity to be markers of intelligence. If we tested a sample of people from this culture on the WAIS and compared their data to data obtained from the Americans, then would we really be studying cross-cultural differences in intelligence? The answer is yes, but only to the extent that we have arbitrarily defined what intelligence is. Suppose a culture considers the ability to have smooth, conflict-free interpersonal relationships to be intelligence. Another culture may consider creativity and artistic abilities to be indexes of intelligence. Would comparisons of WAIS data from any of these cultures constitute cross-cultural comparisons of intelligence?

The gist of a recent cross-cultural study of intimacy was that cultures differ in the ways in which they express intimacy (Barnlund, 1989). This makes sense and certainly is an important research finding. Other cross-cultural researchers will want to extend the research in this area. But sooner or later there needs to be a study of cross-cultural similarities and differences in what intimacy *means* in different cultures. If one culture defines intimacy as certain types of acts whereas another defines it as a shared psychological feeling, then it is no wonder that there are differences in the expression of intimacy across cultures. The real question is, are the observed differences due to differences in the expression of a concept on which both cultures agree, or are the observed differences due to differences in the meaning of the concept itself?

Item Equivalence

Suppose you plan to use a questionnaire that measures intimacy. Most likely, the questionnaire was developed in the United States for use with American subjects. Like all questionnaires, your questionnaire has multiple items. In cross-cultural research, we need to be concerned with whether or not the items mean exactly the same thing in all cultures surveyed. This concern applies not only to the test as a whole, but also to each and every item on the test.

Often, multiple items on a single test are included so that they can collectively "capture" the essence of the variable being measured. These items may be repeated questions of a similar nature, designed to obtain a stable assessment of the variable. For example, in a memory task a subject may be asked to read not one but three stories, each of which contains not one but ten sentences. Then the subject may have to re-create each of the sentences in each story to the best degree possible. It is not adequate to ask just once; multiple-item assessment is a tried and true way of establishing psychometric reliability in measurement.

But what if the items mean different things in different cultures? In measuring vocabulary or general comprehension, a questionnaire may ask what a violin is, or when President's Day is celebrated. Suppose, however, those questions are asked in a culture that does not include violins or other orchestral instruments, and doesn't care, much less know, when Americans celebrate the birthdays of Washington and Lincoln? We need to establish the cultural differences in the details of these types of items in order to find meaningful differences in the concept being measured.

In studying cultural differences in emotion, we might ask subjects to rate how strongly they would feel different emotions in five different contexts. We could trust the findings of such a study only if each of the contexts means the same thing in each culture assessed.

If each item does not mean the same thing in all cultures included in the research, then it is impossible for the researchers to know what they are measuring in the different cultures. And if the researchers are measuring different things in different cultures, then the results obtained are not really comparable.

Subscale and Factor Equivalence

Multiple-item questionnaires often are separated into different parts called scales or subscales. Generally, these scales measure different aspects of the same general variable. The WAIS, for instance, is a multiple-scale test that has verbal subscales (vocabulary, memory, and so on) as well as performance subscales (digit symbol, picture arrangement, and so on). Questionnaire tests such as the Minnesota Multiphasic Personality Inventory (MMPI) and the California Psychological Inventory (CPI) can also contain hundreds of items and many different subscales.

Subscales on a questionnaire are sometimes determined by theoretical considerations. That is, a researcher looks over the questionnaire and makes decisions based on conceptual understanding of subgroups that should exist in the questionnaire. More often, however, subscale determination is made by a statistical procedure known as *factor analysis.*

In short, factor analysis allows a researcher to group multiple items on a questionnaire based on the interrelationships among the items. There are several different types of factor analyses; the one most commonly used is called principal components factors analysis with Varimax rotation. What is important about this technique as it relates to this discussion is that it produces groupings of the items on a test that are statistically independent of each other. Researchers look at these groupings and determine whether the items that group together make sense or not—that is, whether the items all seem to be measuring some key, underlying concept. If they do, researchers say that the factors are *interpretable* and give the underlying concept a name, called a *factor label.*

In this way, a multiple-item test of, say, 50 items can be reduced to a three- or four-subscale (groupings) test, each with some number of specific items (for example, 5 to 15). Not only is there efficiency in the reduction in the data, but there is also built-in reliability because, as was mentioned earlier, multiple-item assessments are more reliable than single items.

Although many researchers are thorough in developing measures with such care and concern in the United States with

American samples, this type of factor and scale determination does not often occur in cross-cultural research. Aside from the problems of concept and item equivalence described earlier, there is a good possibility that different cultures will produce different subscales on the same type of test, or that they will produce no interpretable subscales.

Clearly, it is important to ascertain whether the people of different cultures in a study are treating the questionnaire in the ways intended, and whether scale and factor scores mean the same thing to all the subjects involved. To resolve these questions, researchers can recreate the factor analyses done in the United States on the data obtained in another culture (for example, Brazil). If the same items are associated in the same groupings as in the data from the United States, then we would have some assurance that the same underlying constructs are being measured and that they are being measured by the same items. If, however, items in the re-created factor analyses are associated in different groupings or the groupings do not make sense, then it is quite clear that different things are being measured. In that case, it would be very difficult to justify scoring the test and making interpretations from it in the same way one would with an American sample.

Unfortunately, many cross-cultural studies are not as thorough as they should be with regard to measure equivalence. Researchers conducting studies with other cultures often use tests developed in the United States and show little concern for these issues. They assume not only that the questionnaire measures the same concept, but also that the items on the test, and the subfactor groupings of the test, are all the same. This is indeed a very *large* assumption. If the assumption happens to be correct, then the researchers are lucky and the data are comparable. If the assumption is incorrect, then the research findings are questionable. Perhaps the biggest problem is that we are operating on assumptions and we don't realize it!

There is also an even subtler problem with respect to factor equivalence. The different subgroups or factors that emerge from a factor analysis are associated with different percentages of the total variability in the data set (represented by *eigenvalues*). The first factor or grouping that emerges is associated with the largest percentage of variability in the data set, the second factor or grouping with the second highest percentage, and so forth. Herein lies the source of another cultural difference.

Factor analyses of a questionnaire taken in two cultures may produce the same number of factors and the same items associated with each factor. But the percentage of the total variability associated with each factor may be different. The factor grouping associated with the largest percentage of variability for the American data may be associated with only the second or third largest percentage for another culture. Conversely, a factor that is second or third largest for the Americans may be the largest for the other culture.

A few years ago, Matsumoto and Kudoh (1987) conducted a factor analytic study of a scale known as the Semantic Differential Scale (Mehrabian, 1972). This scale consists of 18 items that are grouped into three scales (six items each): pleasantness, arousal, and dominance. This grouping was determined by factor analysis conducted earlier on data collected from American subjects. We administered this test to subjects in the United States and Japan and conducted separate factor analyses on the data. We found that the same items were associated with the same groupings in Japan as in the United States. However, we also found that the groupings were associated with different percentages of the total variability in the data set. For the American subjects, arousal was associated with the largest percentage, whereas pleasantness was second. For the Japanese, however, pleasantness was associated with the largest percentage, whereas arousal was second.

These findings clearly indicate that there is *structural* equivalence in the data. That is, the same items are associated with the same groupings in the United States and Japan. Thus, we can score and interpret the meanings of the individual scales in the same way. However, there are differences in the scales in the degree of *primacy* across the cultures. For the American sample, arousal appeared to be a more primary dimension of judgment, whereas for the Japanese, pleasantness appeared to be a more primary dimension. This measurement difference is quite subtle, given the structural equivalence in the test across the two cultures.

Language and Translation Issues

An aspect of measurement that is truly unique to cross-cultural research concerns the language of the questionnaire. Cross-cultural research generally cannot be conducted only in English. If you were to compare the responses of an American sample to those from Beijing, you would need to have both an English and a Chinese version of the questionnaire. How are we to know that the questionnaires themselves are equivalent?

Cross-cultural researchers frequently use a procedure known as *back translation* to ensure some type of equivalence in their research protocols. Back translation involves taking the protocol in one language, translating it to the other, and having someone else translate it back to the original language. If the back-translated version is the same as the original, then some type of equivalence exists. If it is not, then the procedure is repeated until the back-translated version is exactly the same as the original.

The concept underlying this procedure is that the end-product must be a translation equivalent of the original English. The original English is "decentered" through this process (Brislin, 1993), and any culture-specific concepts of the English version are either eliminated or translated equivalently into the target language.

Still, even if the words being used in the two languages are the same, there is no guarantee that those words have exactly the same meanings, with the same nuances, in the two cultures. If the English word *anger*, for example, is translated into another language, we may indeed find the best translation equivalent. But will it have the same connotations, strength, and interpretation in that language that *anger* has in English?

Cross-cultural researchers need to deal with issues of language equivalence so that these factors are not confused with any cultural differences they want to test. "Perfect" equivalence cannot be found between any two languages, and this fact should be considered when evaluating cross-cultural research.

Summary

Not only do researchers need to think critically about possible cultural differences in the conceptual definitions of different variables of interest in cross-cultural research, they also have to examine in detail the exact methods used to measure those variables, down to the very wording of the individual items on the tests. Cultural differences in the conceptual definitions of variables and their measurement are very likely, and as consumers of research we need to be aware of these possibilities.

Environmental, Setting, and Procedural Issues in Cross-Cultural Research

In many of the universities across the United States, students enrolled in introductory classes are required to participate as research subjects in partial fulfillment of class requirements. Because this is an established institution, there is a certain expectation of students, at least in the United States, to participate in research as part of their academic experience. Indeed, many American students are "research-wise," knowing their rights as subjects in experiments, expecting to participate in research, and so on.

Many other countries, however, do not have this custom. In some countries, students are simply forced to participate in research because the professor of the class wants to collect the data. In some countries, students are required to come to a research laboratory; therefore, just coming to a university laboratory for an experiment can have different meanings across cultures.

All the decisions that researchers make in any type of study that we described in Chapter 2 are made in cross-cultural studies as well. However, those decisions can mean different things in different countries. Laboratory or field, day or night, questionnaire or behavior observation—different types of decisions can have different meanings in different cultures. Even the cultural/ethnic/racial "match" between the subjects and the experimenters needs to be considered. Cross-cultural researchers need to confront these differences in their work; we need to be aware of these differences when evaluating cross-cultural research.

4

⌒

Cultural Influences on
Data Analysis and the
Interpretation of Findings

Cross-Cultural Issues in Analyzing Data

Many cross-cultural researchers believe, and rightly so, that most issues in cross-cultural research concern methodology. The sheer amount of information we have so far discussed is an indication of that emphasis in thinking about cultural influences on research. In fact, it may be difficult to think about how culture can influence the way we analyze data other than through our methodology.

Indeed, cultural differences in the use of scales can and do have implications for the way we analyze data from cross-cultural studies. The primary reason for considering culture when analyzing data has to do with a phenomenon known as *cultural response sets*. The existence of cultural response sets has direct implications for the analysis and interpretation of both nominal and scalar data from cross-cultural studies. Although it is true that cultural response sets are a methodological issue to a large degree, we discuss them in this section because of their direct relevance to data analysis.

What Are Cultural Response Sets?

A *cultural response set* is a cultural tendency to respond a certain way on tests or response scales. Data obtained from any culture may be just as reflective of response sets as of the underlying tendency the research is trying to measure.

Response sets are intimately related to culture. After all, making ratings on a scale is a behavior like any other, and culture influences this behavior just as it influences other behaviors. In the United States, we generally consider questionnaires to be rather innocuous and comfortably place our responses along the scale wherever best describes how we truly think and feel. This attitude and behavior are definitely related to the American culture's emphasis on the development of unique, separate individuals and the protection of the rights of individuals in American culture to think, act, and thus respond, in any way.

People in other cultures are influenced by their own cultural backgrounds, just as Americans are by theirs. However, the influences of other cultures are different. For example, some cultures do not foster the development of unique, separate individuals. Instead, these "collectivistic" cultures foster a "tightening" of people around norms. They frown upon individualistic and idiosyncratic behavior and instead encourage adherence to group norm and consensus. In the United States we think that all people are created equal and that we are free or even encouraged to develop our own individual talents. In collectivistic cultures, in contrast, it is thought that the "nail that sticks out gets pounded down."

One influence of collectivistic cultures may be to discourage the use of the ends of bipolar response scales. Bipolar scales are scales that have two opposites—for example, pleasant–unpleasant, good–bad—with a quantitative rating between them. Subjects are often asked to place their response in the space on the scale between the two opposite anchors to show how they feel. A person from a collectivistic culture may hesitate to respond at either extreme of the scale, preferring instead to use more of the middle range. A person from an individualistic culture may not be so hesitant to respond at the extremes.

Cultural differences in response sets may affect bipolar scales, as just described, unipolar scales, forced choice, nominal scales—just about any type of scale. For example, suppose participants in the United States and Hong Kong are asked to judge the intensity of a certain stimulus, using a 7-point scale. When examining the data, the researcher finds that the Americans generally scored around 6 or 7, whereas the people from Hong Kong generally scored around 4 or 5. The researcher may then interpret the finding to mean that the Americans perceived more intensity in the stimuli than did the people from Hong Kong. However, what if the people from Hong Kong actually rate *everything* lower than do the Americans, not just these stimuli?

What if they actually perceive a considerable amount of intensity in the stimuli but have a cultural tendency to use the lower part of the scale?

Cultural response sets may confound the cultural differences observed in data. When both cultural differences *and* response sets are operating, we don't know whether the differences found are reflective of "true" differences between the cultures, or whether they are "just" reflective of response set tendencies. As the quotation marks indicate, on some level, response sets are indeed part and parcel of cultural differences. In our attempts to uncover differences between cultures, however, we need to use whatever means are available to specify exactly what source contributes to the differences observed—response set tendencies or otherwise.

Cultural response sets are not necessarily operating in *all* cross-cultural data; in fact, many times they are probably not influencing the data. However, just the *possibility* that cultural response sets are at work means that the researcher needs to look for them. If the researcher finds evidence that the data may be influenced by them, then this problem must be resolved and the interpretations adjusted accordingly.

Fortunately, there are statistical manipulations that researchers can use to deal with the possible influences of cultural response sets. In the next sections we discuss different analytic techniques for dealing with cultural response sets—one for quantitative scalar data, the other for nominal data.

Dealing with Cultural Response Set Influences on Continuous Data

Some General Issues

Continuous data are quantitative and classified as ordinal, interval, or ratio scales of measurement. When dealing with continuous data from different cultures, we can observe cultural differences in response set tendencies in different ways.

One of the easiest ways to see response set tendencies in continuous data is mean differences. If, for example, the means from two (or more) cultures are different from each other, then it is possible that one or both of those means were influenced by a cultural tendency to use only part of the scale.

Wait a minute! Mean differences may be reflective of cultural response set differences? Aren't mean differences exactly what we would be looking for in a cross-cultural comparison?

Well, of course we would be looking for group differences in the means in a cross-cultural study using continuous data. However, we cannot escape the possibility that cultural differences in response set tendencies may have influenced the data in such a way to help produce mean differences. Cultural response sets affect not only analysis of the data, but also interpretation of the findings. Research results that merely show mean differences in raw score, continuous data in a single factor design must be interpreted with an awareness of cultural response sets.

Cultural differences in response tendencies can influence continuous data in other ways as well. For example, if cultural response sets exist for a certain culture, then not only would the ratings tend to center on a certain value (such as the mean), but also the variance of the ratings from that culture would be smaller. That is, the variability associated with those ratings will probably be smaller if cultural response sets are operative.

Differences in cultural response tendencies that produce differences not only in means but also in variances tend to complicate the analysis of cross-cultural data.

Analysis of a Single-Factor Experiment

Suppose you have conducted a simple, cross-cultural experiment on people's values about sharing goods, ideas, and products with other people.[1] Your study was a three-culture study involving respondents from the United States, Russia, and South Korea. Ten subjects in each culture were given a simple questionnaire on which they were asked to rate how important they

---

[1]Actually, this hypothetical example is based on several recent studies conducted in my laboratory on cultural similarities and differences in individualistic and collectivistic tendencies in social behaviors (Matsumoto et al., 1993; Preston et al., 1993; Weissman et al., 1992). The data used in this example are entirely fictitious. They do, however, highlight how cultural response sets may be operative in a data set and the methods and techniques used to tease them out. Interested readers can contact our laboratory for copies of the full reports of the actual studies to see how these were handled in reality. (Write to Intercultural and Emotion Research Laboratory, Department of Psychology, San Francisco State University, 1600 Holloway Avenue, San Francisco, CA 94132.)

believe it is for them to share their goods, ideas, and other material and nonmaterial possessions with other members of their family. In making their ratings, the subjects in all three cultures were asked to use a 7-point rating scale, from "not at all important to me" (0) to "extremely important to me" (6).[2] The data from this study are reported in Table 1. Take a moment now to look these data over.

As you can see from the descriptive statistics presented for each culture, the Russians had the highest ratings, the South Koreans the second highest, and the Americans the lowest. If you tested the differences among the three cultures on these data using a single factor, between subjects analysis of variance (ANOVA), you would obtain the ANOVA findings summarized at the bottom of Table 1. The significant F ratio obtained in the ANOVA on these data indicates that the cultures do indeed differ in their ratings of the importance of sharing.

Following up on the significant overall F ratio, let's compute some analytic comparisons. Suppose we test the difference between the pairs of cultures, again using the F ratio. We would obtain the following results:

- The ratings by the Russians were significantly higher than the ratings by the Americans, $F(1,27) = 10.24, p < .001$.
- The ratings by the South Koreans also were significantly higher than the ratings by the Americans, $F(1,27) = 6.76, p < .01$.
- There was no difference between the ratings made by the Russians and those made by the South Koreans, $F(1,27) = .36$, ns.[3]

---

[2] Of course, the study just described presents many of the pitfalls of doing cross-cultural work described in this book. Supposing that cultural differences underlie the countries is a major assumption, regardless of how safe that assumption may appear. Supposing that the ten subjects from each culture are adequate representatives of those cultures is yet another major assumption. We acknowledge these and other problems in this hypothetical study now, drawing attention instead to the types of issues the data from this study may raise in terms of response sets and data analysis.

[3] These analytic comparisons were computed using the procedures outlined by Keppel and Saufley (1980). These procedures involved the computation of the comparison sum of squares using coefficients, and the use of the within groups error term as the denominator in all the comparisons. Other statistical procedures would most likely yield very similar, although not exactly the same results. Differences in statistical technique are not important at this point, however.

Table 1
An Example of Cultural Differences in a Questionnaire Rating: Family

	Culture		
	United States	Russia	South Korea
	3	5	4
	4	5	5
	4	5	6
	2	4	2
	6	6	4
	4	5	4
	1	5	6
	3	4	5
	2	4	5
	3	5	4
Means	3.20	4.80	4.50
sd	1.40	.64	1.18

Analysis of Variance Summary Table				
Source	Sum of Squares	df	Mean Squares	F Ratio
Culture (between groups)	14.47	2	7.23	5.80**
Error (within groups)	33.70	27	1.25	
Total	48.17	29		

$**p < .01$

Although these findings are provocative, there is also evidence
that cultural response sets are contributing to these data. The
very fact that the means are different between the cultures, for
example, suggests that response sets may be operative. The Russians and the South Koreans may have used the higher end of
the scale because of the way the scale is worded or constructed,
or just because that's the way they use scales. The Americans
may have used the lower end of the scale for similar reasons.
Regardless of how the cultural response sets may be interfering
with these data, however, there is no good way to deal with

them. It would be helpful to conduct other studies in which respondents from these same cultures rate something else using a similar scale; then we could see whether the respondents use the scales similarly with other types of ratings.

There is yet another consideration: cultural response sets may also be observed in differences in variance. The variance associated with the data from each culture is represented by the square of the standard deviation (sd). If you look closely at the standard deviations shown in Table 1, you will see that the variance of the Russian data is considerably smaller than that for either the Americans or the South Koreans.

In fact, we can statistically test the differences between the variances associated with the data from each of the cultures using the F ratio. To do this, we must be sure that we are dealing with variance, not standard deviation; in this example, we square the standard deviation from each of the cultures to obtain the variances: 1.96, .41, and 1.39 for the United States, Russia, and South Korea, respectively. To test the difference between any two variances, we simply divide the larger one by the smaller one. The resulting F ratio can be compared to a critical value of F determined by the degrees of freedom (df) associated with each variance.

For example, to compare the variance in the American data with the variance in the Russian data, we obtain an F ratio that looks like this:

$$F = \frac{1.96}{0.41} = 4.78$$

The critical value of F at (9,9) degrees of freedom is 3.18 (α = .05). Because the F ratio that we obtained is larger than this critical value, we know that the variance in the American data is significantly greater than the variance associated with the Russian data. This is further evidence that cultural response set tendencies may be operating.[4]

Likewise, we can test the differences between the other pairs of variances. We would find that:

- The South Korean data have a significantly greater variance than the Russian data, $F(9,9) = 3.39$, $p < .05$.

---

[4]Not to mention the problem that unequal variances poses for the validity of the ANOVA (the homogeneity of variance assumption).

- There is no difference between the variances for the South Koreans and the Americans, $F(9,9)$ = 1.41, ns.

The ability to test not only the means associated with data from different cultures, but also the variances, gives us more statistical tools with which we can formally test the influence of cultural response tendencies. *When a researcher finds evidence that such tendencies are operating in the data set, the conclusions and interpretations about the findings should allow for these influences.*

For comparison purposes, Table 2 provides another set of data from the same hypothetical experiment. You will see that the means are exactly the same as those shown in Table 1. In addition, the overall ANOVA findings are similar, as are the analytic, follow-up comparisons. The only difference between these two data sets is in the variability associated with the Russian data. The variance associated with the Russian data in Table 2 is larger than in Table 1. Thus, in these data there is no evidence for the cultural response sets in variability of response.[5]

Analysis of a Two-Factor Experiment

When cross-cultural data are obtained from a two-factor or multifactor experiment, the possibilities with regard to data analysis increase. Let's say, for example, that the study described previously was part of a larger study, and that another part of that study involved ten other subjects in each culture making similar ratings. These subjects, however, rated how important it was for them to share their things with strangers (remember, the first group of subjects rated the value of sharing things with family members). The data from this second group of subjects, as well as the ANOVA findings, are summarized in Table 3. As you can see, there are no significant differences among the American, Russian, and South Korean means in these data.

Actually, because the data in Table 3 are part of a larger experiment, as described earlier, we can combine all the data into a single data set, separated not only by culture, but also by the group being rated (family members or strangers). Thus, we can put all the data into a single table (Table 4), calculating de-

---

[5]There still is the possibility of cultural response sets evidenced in the means, however. Again, nothing can be done about that in this study.

Table 2
Another Example of Cultural Differences in a Questionnaire Rating:
Family

	Culture	
United States	Russia	South Korea
3	6	4
4	5	5
4	5	6
2	3	2
6	6	4
4	5	4
1	5	6
3	5	5
2	2	5
3	6	4

Means	3.20	4.80	4.50
sd	1.40	1.32	1.18

Analysis of Variance Summary Table

Source	Sum of Squares	df	Mean Squares	F Ratio
Culture (between groups)	14.47	2	7.23	4.27*
Error (within groups)	45.70	27	1.69	
Total	60.17	29		

*$p < .5$

scriptive statistics for each social group and then across both social groups.[6]

When there is evidence that cultural response sets may be operating and continuous data on the same type of rating from a two- or multifactor experiment are available, one option for

---

[6]For the remainder of this example, we will be using the data from Table 2, which shows approximately equal variances in the data from all three cultures.

Table 3
Cultural Differences in a Questionnaire Rating: Strangers

	Culture		
	United States	Russia	South Korea
	1	0	0
	2	2	0
	3	2	3
	4	3	3
	0	4	2
	2	0	1
	2	1	1
	0	2	3
	3	1	2
	3	3	4
Means	2.00	1.80	1.90
sd	1.33	1.32	1.37

Analysis of Variance Summary Table				
Source	Sum of Squares	df	Mean Squares	F Ratio
Culture (between groups)	.20	2	.10	.06
Error (within groups)	48.50	27	1.80	
Total	48.70	29		

analyzing that data is to convert all the scores into standardized scores *within each culture*. (This is *not* an option when dealing with data from a single-factor study. Can you see why?)

For Table 5, we have taken the data from Table 4 and converted each score into a standardized score (z), using the formula

$$z = \frac{(X - \overline{X})}{sd}$$

Table 4
Combining the Data on Family and Strangers

	Culture		
	United States	Russia	South Korea
Family	3	6	4
	4	5	5
	4	5	6
	2	3	2
	6	6	4
	4	5	4
	1	5	6
	3	5	5
	2	2	5
	3	6	4
Means	3.20	4.80	4.50
sd	1.40	1.32	1.18
Strangers	1	0	0
	2	2	0
	3	2	3
	4	3	3
	0	4	2
	2	0	1
	2	1	1
	0	2	3
	3	1	2
	3	3	4
Means	2.00	1.80	1.90
sd	1.33	1.32	1.37
Overall Means	2.60	3.30	3.20
Overall sd	1.47	2.00	1.82

Thus, for example, the first score for the American data for family members was computed as follows:

$$z = \frac{(3.00 - 2.60)}{1.47} = +.27$$

Table 5
Data Converted to Standardized Scores

| | Culture | | |
	United States	Russia	South Korea
Family	.27	1.35	.44
	.96	.85	.99
	.96	.85	.54
	−.41	−.15	−.66
	2.32	1.35	.44
	.96	.85	.44
	−1.09	.85	1.54
	.27	.85	.99
	−.41	−.65	.99
	.27	1.35	.44
Means	.41	.75	.71
sd	.95	.66	.65
Strangers	−1.09	−1.65	−1.75
	−.41	−.65	−1.75
	.27	−.65	−.11
	.96	−.15	−.11
	−1.77	.35	−.66
	−.41	−1.65	−1.21
	−.41	−1.15	−1.21
	−1.77	−.65	−.11
	.27	−1.15	−.66
	.27	−.15	.44
Means	−.41	−.75	−.71
sd	.91	.66	.75
Overall Means	.00	.00	.00
Overall sd	1.00	1.00	1.00

As you can see, we are using the overall mean from both data sets (2.60) and the overall standard deviation (1.47). This ensures that the data are standardized within the culture, keeping intact any within-culture differences.

In similar fashion, the remaining scores were standardized using the overall means and standard deviations from each respective culture. Because they are standardized scores, some are positive, some negative. Standardizing the data within each culture produces an overall mean of 0 and an overall standard deviation of 1, as seen in the bottom summary in Table 5. But, the standardization preserves any subgroup mean differences that exist, as shown in the subgroup descriptives for each culture.

We then recomputed the ANOVAs presented earlier, separately for family members and strangers, but this time on the standardized data in Table 5. The summaries of these analyses are presented in Table 6.

As you can see, neither of the analyses produced any statistically significant results. This is in contrast to the results found with raw scores. Remember, the raw score analyses produced cultural differences in the ratings for family members, with Russian and South Korean subjects giving significantly higher ratings than the Americans. When the scores are converted to standardized scores, however, and the analyses are repeated, the differences do not exist.

It is important to realize that this does not mean that one analysis is correct and the other is wrong. They are both equally valid, important, and interesting analysis plans. The raw score analyses indicate what the differences are in the original units that were measured. Although these measurements may be confounded by cultural response sets, they are important because these differences reflect what we would expect to see in actual behaviors or reports of ratings. The standardized score analyses, however, transform the raw data so that they reflect individual differences *relative to their own culture*. To understand and interpret the findings, it is crucial to recognize that standardized scores reflect the raw data but do so relative to culture.

In this example, the findings on the standardized data indicate that there are *no* differences between the cultures *when the data are represented relative to their own average*. The difference between the raw score analyses and the standardized score analyses reflect important considerations in how we are to

Table 6
Analyses of Variance on Standardized Data

Analysis of Variance Summary Table				
Family				
Source	Sum of Squares	df	Mean Squares	F Ratio
Culture (between groups)	.69	2	.35	.59
Error (within groups)	15.85	27	.59	
Total	16.54	29		

Analysis of Variance Summary Table				
Strangers				
Source	Sum of Squares	df	Mean Squares	F Ratio
Culture (between groups)	.69	2	.35	.57
Error (within groups)	16.42	27	.61	
Total	17.12	29		

interpret cultural differences and the reasons that they exist. In this example, there really are no differences between the cultures when we consider the data relative to themselves![7]

Standardizing data from multifactor, cross-cultural studies is generally a good idea, regardless of any evidence of cultural response sets. The only thing that we cannot test is the overall cultural differences in the means, because all the means are transformed to 0 by default. (That is why we cannot consider standardizing data from a single-factor experiment; all the means

---

[7]Actually, there are many ways to attack this data set. One option, for example, would be to start with a two-factor ANOVA, using culture and social group as the independent variables, and then follow up with specific, analytic comparisons. Other analysis plans also exist. Regardless of the plan, the emphasis here is on the standardization of the data and on re-creating analyses in addition to analyses with only raw score data.

would be transformed to 0, and there would be nothing to test!) Other than that particular comparison, however, all other comparisons can be conducted. The only difference between these analyses and raw score analyses is that the standardized data have been "corrected" relative to themselves. Remember, to standardize data, the data must be obtained from a multifactor study and be on the same scale of measurement.

A final note about standardizing data to eliminate cultural response sets: The example provided here showed a difference in raw score analyses that disappeared in standardized analyses. This, of course, can and does happen with actual data. There are many possible outcomes. Findings may come and go; differences will disappear and reoccur. All possible permutations of findings between raw score and standardized data may be found. Again, there is not *one* right technique. Both are right. The important point is to make sense of the *pattern* of obtained results, especially if the results are different for raw as opposed to standardized scores.

Dealing with Cultural Response Set Influences on Nominal Data

Cultural response sets can affect not only continuous data from a cross-cultural study, but nominal data as well. The issues concerning nominal data, however, are slightly different.

Let's take as an example a study conducted on cultural differences in communication when interacting with people of differing status (Tomioka, 1993). Subjects in different cultures were asked to respond to a questionnaire in which they were to report how they interacted with people of higher, lower, or the same status as themselves. The questions concerned introductions, clothing, verbal and nonverbal behaviors, disclosures of work-related behaviors, and disclosures of personal and family issues.

We have selected some questions from the study to demonstrate cultural response tendencies with nominal data. As you can see in Table 7, subjects were asked to check off as many items in each group of behaviors as they thought would apply to them. Although all these questions were asked of interactions with people of three different status levels, for demonstration

Table 7
Sample Questions Generating Nominal Data

Instructions: Please recall your most recent first encounter with someone else whom you did not know previously or you did not speak to previously and whom you perceived to be of higher status, such as superiors or bosses. The situation can be either a one-to-one setting or a small-group setting. In the case of a small-group setting, focus on one person. You may check multiple boxes for a single question. Please check off your responses.

Which of the following behaviors did you do during your encounter?

I. Distance and Posture

[   ]   a.   Sat or stood with a forward lean
[   ]   b.   Sat or stood straight back
[   ]   c.   Sat or stood with a backward lean
[   ]   d.   Sat or stood close to the other person

II. Work-Related Information

[   ]   a.   Mentioned where I work
[   ]   b.   Mentioned the kind of organization
[   ]   c.   Mentioned my company's name
[   ]   d.   Mentioned my section/division/department
[   ]   e.   Mentioned my occupation in general
[   ]   f.   Mentioned the specific work I do
[   ]   g.   Mentioned how long I have worked for this company
[   ]   h.   Mentioned former jobs
[   ]   i.   Mentioned what I liked about my job
[   ]   j.   Mentioned what I dislike about my job
[   ]   k.   Mentioned what I dislike about my company
[   ]   l.   Mentioned mutual acquaintances we may have
[   ]   m.   Mentioned my future goals
[   ]   n.   Mentioned my opinion and feelings on issues

III. My Responsibilities

[   ]   a.   Did not talk about my responsibilities
[   ]   b.   Mentioned my responsibilities ambiguously
[   ]   c.   Understated my responsibilities
[   ]   d.   Mentioned my responsibilities objectively
[   ]   e.   Stressed my responsibilities
[   ]   f.   Someone else described my responsibilities for me

Table 8
*Sample Frequency Data and Chi-Squares from
the First Group of Questions*

I. Distance and Posture Questions

	United States	Hong Kong	Chi-Square
a.	25	30	.45
b.	24	32	1.14
c.	37	12	12.76***
d.	41	15	12.07***

***$p < .001$

purposes here let's assume that the ratings were made only in relation to interactions with a higher-status person.

The data generated from this questionnaire are basically dichotomous, nominal data. That is, respondents simply check off each behavior that describes what happened during their interactions. Thus, the basic data are dichotomous—checked or not checked. These data are fundamentally different from the rating scales described in earlier examples.

In the study, respondents from two cultures (say, the United States and Hong Kong) were asked to complete the questionnaires.[8] The basic data in this study are frequencies— that is, the number of people that checked off each particular behavior. Differences between the two cultures can be tested using chi-square, computing it separately for each particular behavior. Table 8 shows the frequency data and chi-squares for the first set of questions on distance and posture. Note that these chi-square computations can be done on *all* the questions, not just the first group.

The data in Table 8 indicate that there were no differences between the Americans and Chinese on the first two questions. Significantly more Americans, however, checked off the last two questions of this group than did the Chinese. We might conclude that Americans are more likely than Chinese to sit or stand

---

[8]Actually, in Tomioka's (1993) study, the two cultures were the United States and Japan.

with a backward lean and closer to a higher-status person when interacting with that person.

But wait! These are not the only differences that may exist in the data set. Cultural response sets may also be producing other differences. With nominal data, cultural response sets may be seen in the tendency to check off the behaviors described. Some cultures may encourage respondents to check off many behaviors; in other cultures respondents may be more hesitant to respond on these types of scales. Differences observed on any single item or question may reflect not only actual cultural differences in behaviors, but also tendencies to check off more items when responding to such scales!

One way to check whether such tendencies exist would be to count the number of responses each subject gave to all the questions, and then to compare the average number of responses for one culture against that for another. If people of one culture, on the average, simply give more responses than people of another, then cultural response sets may be at work.

We did exactly that in our example. First, we counted the number of responses each person gave to the four questions from the first group of questions.[9] Thus, each person can have a score from 0 (no item checked) to 4 (all items checked). Then we produced descriptive statistics (means and standard deviations) for these response scores across subjects for each culture. An ANOVA was computed on the response scores, using culture as a single, between-subjects independent variable. The results are reported in Table 9.

As you can see, the F ratio was significant, indicating that the Americans had a significantly higher mean than did the Chinese. This is evidence of a possible cultural tendency to respond more freely on this type of questionnaire. Americans may simply check off more things, and the differences observed in Table 8 may actually reflect cultural differences in response tendencies as well as cultural differences in actual behavior.

---

[9] You can do this for single groups of questions, as we are doing in this example, or for all the questions and items that the subjects responded to. The latter, in fact, would probably be a better indicator of overall response tendencies. In this example, however, we will use only the data from the first group of questions.

Table 9
Response Data across Questions

I. Distance and Posture Questions

	United States	Hong Kong
Mean Responses	2.3	1.8
sd	1.1	1.2

Analysis of Variance Summary Table

Source	Sum of Squares	df	Mean Squares	F Ratio
Culture (between groups)	6.27	1	6.27	4.71*
Error (within groups)	63.84	48	1.33	
Total	70.11	49		

*$p < .05$

Which interpretation is correct? Are there cultural differences in actual behavior, as reported in Table 8? Or are those differences merely differences in cultural response sets, as evidenced in Table 9? Well, the answer is that we don't know. It could be one, or the other, or both. The analyses that we have presented so far about this problem cannot determine unequivocally which is the "correct" interpretation.

As in the cases described earlier of cultural response sets in continuous data, the real goal of these analyses is to provide alternative hypotheses to explain cultural differences when we find them. If, for example, the data presented in Table 9 did *not* produce a significant F ratio, then we could rule out possible cultural response tendencies. We could then determine that the differences observed in Table 8 are probably reflective of actual cultural differences. If the data indicate possible cultural response sets, however, then both hypotheses are viable until someone conducts other studies to tease out the effects of response sets on these types of judgments in these cultures. The bottom line for this study is that the analyses, if statistically significant, leave us with both possible hypotheses.

Cultural Influences on the Interpretation
of Findings from Cross-Cultural Studies

We have already touched upon several issues concerning interpretations of cultural differences in cross-cultural research. As
we saw earlier, the data analysis from a study may lend itself to
more than one interpretation of the data. One interpretation may
be that the differences are reflective of cultural differences in
actual behavior. Another interpretation may be that those differences reflect cultural response sets. When interpreting and discussing results, the important thing to remember is to give equal
consideration to both (and other) alternatives, finding weight for
one or the other in other research. Although the exact nature of
the difference may be ambiguous, in doing cross-cultural work
we need to be able to tolerate this ambiguity, without falling
into the trap of merely assuming that one interpretation is correct and not the other.

There are many other ways in which culture influences the
interpretation of findings, specifically differences, in a cross-cultural study. Earlier in this book, we discussed how culture can
bias the formulation of the research questions in a cross-cultural
study. Culture can also bias the ways in which researchers interpret findings. Most researchers will inevitably interpret their data
(whether from questionnaires, responses to a task, or something
else) through their own cultural filters. Of course, this bias can
affect the interpretation in varying degrees. Interpretation of
group differences in means, for example, may simply indicate
differences in degrees. If the mean response for Americans on a
rating scale, for instance, is 6.0 and the mean for Hong Kong
Chinese is 4.0, then one interpretation is that the Americans simply scored higher on the scale. Another interpretation may be
that the Chinese are suppressing their responses.

The second interpretation is common. But how do we
know the Chinese are suppressing their responses? What if the
Americans are exaggerating their responses? What if the Chinese
mean response of 4.0 is actually the more "correct" one, and the
American mean is the one that is off? What if we surveyed the
rest of the world and found that the mean for the rest of the
world is actually 3.0, and that *both* the Chinese and the Americans inflated their ratings somehow? What if the differences oc-

curred only because the question being asked was more important to one culture than to the other?

Examples such as this one are found throughout the cross-cultural literature. Whenever researchers make a *value* interpretation of a finding, there is always the possibility that the interpretation is bound by a cultural bias. Interpretations of good or bad, right or wrong, suppressing or exaggerating, important or unimportant—these are all value interpretations that in a cross-cultural study may reflect the value orientations of the researchers as much as they do the cultures of the samples included in the study.

A final word about cultural differences in the interpretation of research findings concerns the value that people in different cultures place on research findings. In the United States, Americans are quite research oriented, placing high value on the findings from research and the implications of those findings for our lives—especially for making changes in our lives (think about research documenting relationships between smoking and lung cancer, or cholesterol and heart disease). People of many other cultures, however, do not hold research findings in such high regard. They may believe the findings, but it is yet another leap to make changes in their lives because of them. These attitudes about research are directly related to attributions of responsibility and control over events and behaviors. Cultures influence how people think about responsibility and control issues, and these, in turn, affect the importance of research findings to those people.

Summary

Many issues complicate the conduct and evaluation of cross-cultural research. These issues have probably discouraged some researchers from conducting cross-cultural studies, which is unfortunate. Recognizing and understanding these issues are not only important to conducting cross-cultural research; they are also important first steps in appreciating cultural differences.

5

_ᴑ_

Tips for Conducting Your
Own Cross-Cultural Study

After reviewing all the pitfalls and issues described in this book, you're probably wondering why anyone should conduct any type of cross-cultural research. You can probably find fault with all cross-cultural studies—in the formulation of the questions, the methodology, the data analysis, the interpretation. The picture looks pretty bleak.

Despite all these difficulties, however, we need to conduct cross-cultural studies. When we read about others' studies, not only do we need to find the problems and concerns that detract from the study, we also need to find all those things that are right with the study and glean from it everything that we reasonably can. Only by conducting and reviewing cross-cultural research can we learn about cultural influences on human behavior. We cannot postpone our studies until we can conduct the "perfect" study; if we do, we will be waiting a long, long time. We must continue to conduct cross-cultural studies, hopefully addressing the concerns and issues outlined in this book.

So now you're pumped up and eager to conduct your own cross-cultural study, right? _Great!_ Of course, the first thing you should do is read, or reread, this book, and take from it whatever knowledge or information you can about conducting your study. In addition, here are some other concrete tips that you should consider.

1. _Ask someone who is knowledgeable about the cultures you are trying to study to collaborate with you on your research._ Even if you can't find a continuous collaborator, find some consultants who can give you advice, test your assumptions about what you are trying to do, and help you develop data analysis

plans and interpret the findings in ways that you may not have considered.

2. *Get a full demographic assessment of all your subjects in all your cultures.* All too often, we are comfortable about getting information only on age, gender, and perhaps ethnicity. In your study you should try to get as comprehensive a demographics assessment as possible, including these variables: place of birth and upbringing, religious backgrounds, occupation, socioeconomic status, and so on. All these social influences may confound the cultural groupings. It is important to be able to tease out effects due to these influences, even if it is impossible to control these factors absolutely.

3. *Search for measures that have psychometric reliability and validity for all your subjects.* Very few measures have been validated in different cultures. If the one you want to use has been, then use it. If not, you may want to do some method development prior to conducting your main study. That development could include pretesting measures, items, tasks, and so on. If you are developing your own questionnaire, give some thought to simultaneous parallel forms development in both cultures.

4. *Run a pilot study.* After you think you have determined everything you want to do in your study, translated all your protocols, and what not, run a small pilot study in both cultures before conducting the main study. After the pilot, engage your subjects in discussions about their experiences in the study. After that, sit down with your collaborators and discuss not only the efficacy of the procedures but also the reactions of the subjects. Make adjustments along the way.

5. *Develop a "culture-free" analysis plan that involves raw score as well as standardized score analyses.* Ask your collaborators to help you develop culture-free analysis plans. These plans should include cultural response sets and "slicing up" the data in many different ways, not only in ways that bias the results for one culture or another.

6. *Have people of different cultural backgrounds check your interpretations of the data.* This is also an important part of research. Your collaborators or consultants can aid in checking and eliminating value-laden interpretations that bias the findings toward one culture over another.

7. *In designing your study and interpreting its results, give some thought to what kinds of underlying psychological dimen-*

sions of culture produced, or should produce, differences. Most of the time, we are interested in conducting cross-cultural research because of our interest in a specific comparison involving one or more specific ethnic or racial groups. You should also consider underlying psychological dimensions of culture that produce differences in the cultures you are interested in as well as in others. Dimensions such as individualism versus collectivism and status differentiation are applicable to all cultures and ethnicities and can be especially helpful in planning studies and interpreting findings. Only in this way can we transform cross-cultural research from the mere accumulation of facts about different cultures to a general understanding of culture in its broadest sense.

We hope that these tips, along with the discussions throughout this book, will help you conduct meaningful cross-cultural research. Just remember, meaningful research is painstakingly detailed and complex. It might be easy to conduct studies that gloss over these issues, but what would they really say?

6

∽

Conclusion

Research is the primary way by which academicians and scholars generate knowledge about the world. The knowledge that we find through the research process, and that is repeatedly found across a number of studies, is said to be replicated. Replicated findings and knowledge form the basis for what we know as "truth" about the world. It is this truth that is taught in schools (we hope), conveyed every day in the classrooms and in books.

As we have discussed here, however, that truth is bounded by the conditions, parameters, and limitations placed on it by the studies and research that produced the knowledge. All studies are bounded in some fashion by these parameters, whether decisions about those conditions are made consciously by the researchers or by default. This is true for research in all social sciences, regardless of field or discipline.

Thus, it is important for researchers, and for consumers of that research, to be aware of what types of conditions and parameters exist and how they limit the knowledge that is produced by research.

Cross-cultural research brings with it its own special set of issues concerning the conditions and parameters of research. Many of these issues are merely extensions of general research issues into the cross-cultural arena. Some issues, however, pertain solely to cross-cultural research. Regardless, in learning about knowledge generated from cross-cultural research, it is imperative to learn about these issues and to be a critical reader and evaluator of the cross-cultural literature.

There are so many issues that the critical reader needs to learn about that you might be wondering right now whether *any* cross-cultural study can tell us *anything*. You may be thinking that there is always something that limits every cross-cultural study, that all studies have some imperfection.

Well, there is no perfect study; every study does have some kind of imperfection. But that does not necessarily mean that we cannot learn something from the study. The real question in thinking about and evaluating cross-cultural research is whether the flaws of a study so outweigh its procedures that they severely compromise the trust that you might place in its data. If a study is so compromised by problems that you don't trust the data, then you shouldn't believe the findings. But if a study's problems are not so severe, then you should be able to glean from it information about cultural differences. If you can do this over a number of studies in an area, then they cumulatively or collectively may say something about that area, even though any single study may not.

This process of evaluating the merits of each and every study in terms of the trust you would place in the data, and then accumulating the bits and pieces of information across the studies you trust, is integral to learning about a field. These are the types of studies that we should learn from and should conduct in the future.

·◯·

References and Resources

References

Barnlund, D. (1989). *Communicative styles of Japanese and Americans: Images and realities.* Belmont, CA: Wadsworth.

Barnouw, V. (1985). *Culture and personality.* Chicago: Dorsey Press.

Brislin, R. (1993). *Understanding culture's influence on behavior.* New York: Harcourt Brace Jovanovich.

Keppel, G., & Saufley, W. H. (1980). *Introduction to design and analysis.* New York: W. H. Freeman.

Matsumoto, D., Brown, B., Preston, K., & Weissman, M. (1993, August). *The need for better measures of individualism-collectivism on the individual level.* Paper presented at a symposium on "Measuring individualism-collectivism on the level of the individual" (D. Matsumoto, Chair) at the Annual Convention of the American Psychological Association, Toronto, Canada.

Matsumoto, D., & Kudoh, T. (1987). Cultural similarities and differences in the semantic dimensions of body postures. *Journal of Nonverbal Behavior, 11,* 166–179.

Mehrabian, A. (1972). *Nonverbal communication.* Chicago: Aldine.

Preston, K., Matsumoto, D., Weissman, M., & Brown, B. (1993, August). *CCAI results from different countries, cultures, and ethnicities.* Paper presented at a symposium on "Measuring individualism-collectivism on the level of the individual" (D. Matsumoto, Chair) at the Annual Convention of the American Psychological Association, Toronto, Canada.

Tomioka, M. (1993). *Communication styles of self-presentation in Japan and the United States.* Unpublished master's thesis, San Francisco State University.

Triandis, H. (1992, February). *Individualism and collectivism as a cultural syndrome.* Paper presented at the Annual Convention of the Society for Cross-Cultural Researchers, Santa Fe, NM.

Weissman, M., Brown, B., Preston, K., Tafe, B., & Matsumoto, D. (1992, April). *The California Cultural Assessment Inventory (CCAI): Developing a measure of individualism-collectivism.* Paper presented at the Western Psychogical Association Annual Conference, Portland, OR.

General Readings on Culture

Barnouw, V. (1985). *Culture and personality.* Chicago: Dorsey Press.

Berry, J. W., Poortinga, Y. H., Segall, M. H., & Dasen, P. R. (1992). *Cross-cultural psychology: Research and applications.* New York: Cambridge University Press.

Brislin, R. (1990). *Applied cross-cultural psychology.* Newbury Park, CA: Sage.

Brislin, R. (1993). *Understanding culture's influence on behavior.* Fort Worth, TX: Harcourt Brace Jovanovich.

Burlew, A. K. H., Banks, W. C., McAdoo, H. P., & Azibo, D. A. (1992). *African American psychology.* Newbury Park, CA: Sage.

Cohen. (1994). *Psychology and adjustment: Values, culture, and change.* Needham Heights, MA: Allyn & Bacon.

Cole, M., & Scribner, S. (1974). *Culture and thought: A psychological introduction.* New York: Wiley.

Eckensberger., L., Lonner, W., & Poortinga, Y. (Eds.). (1979). *Cross-cultural contributions to psychology.* Amsterdam: Swets and Zeitlinger.

Hofstede, G. (1984). *Culture's consequences.* Newbury Park, CA: Sage.

Hofstede, G. (1991). *Cultures and organizations: Software of the mind.* London: McGraw-Hill.

Kagitcibasi, C., & Berry, J. (1989). Cross-cultural psychology: Current research and trends. *Annual Review of Psychology, 40,* 493–531.

Lonner, W., & Malpass, R. (1993). *Psychology and culture.* Needham Heights, MA: Allyn & Bacon.

Marsella, A., Tharp, R., & Ciborowski, T. (1979). *Perspectives on cross-cultural psychology.* New York: Academic Press.

Matsumoto, D. (1994). *People: Psychology from a cultural perspective.* Pacific Grove, CA: Brooks/Cole.

Segall, M. H., Dasen, P., Berry, J., & Poortinga, Y. (1990). *Human behavior in global perspective.* Elmsford, NY: Pergamon Press.

Shweder, R. (1991). *Thinking through cultures: Expeditions in cultural psychology.* Cambridge, MA: Harvard University Press.

Shweder, R., & Levine, R. (1984). *Culture theory.* New York: Cambridge University Press.

Triandis, H. (1972). *The analysis of subjective culture.* New York: Wiley.

Triandis, H. (1994). *Culture and social behavior.* New York: McGraw-Hill.

Triandis, H., Lambert, W., Berry, J., Lonner, W., Heron, A., Brislin, R., & Draguns, J. (Eds.). (1980). *Handbook of cross-cultural psychology* (6 vols.). Boston: Allyn & Bacon.

Readings on Cross-Cultural Research Methods

Asthana, H. S. (1974). A procedure for achieving equivalence of communication in cross-cultural research. *Journal of Social and Economic Studies, 2*, 87–94.

Baldauf, R. B., & Jernudd, B. H. (1986). Aspects of language use in cross-cultural psychology. Special issue: Contributions to cross-cultural psychology. *Australian Journal of Psychology, 38*, 381–392.

Bardo, J. W. (1976). Internal consistency and reliability in Likert-type attitude scales: Some questions concerning the use of pre-built scales. *Sociology and Social Research, 60*, 403–420.

Berry, J. W. (1979). Research in multicultural societies: Implications of cross-cultural methods. *Journal of Cross-Cultural Psychology, 10*, 415.

Berry, J. W. (1989). Imposed etics-emics-derived etics: The operationalization of a compelling idea. Special issue: Cross-cultural comparison of psychological data: Issues and pitfalls. *International Journal of Psychology, 24*, 721–735.

Brislin, R. (1970). Back translation for cross-cultural research. *Journal of Cross-Cultural Psychology, 1*, 185–216.

Brislin, R. W. (1976). Comparative research methodology: Cross-cultural studies. *International Journal of Psychology, 11*, 215–229.

Brislin, R. W. (1983). Cross-cultural research in psychology. *Annual Review of Psychology, 34*, 363–400.

Brislin, R. W., Lonner, W. J., & Thorndike, R. M. (1973). *Cross-cultural research methods*. New York: Wiley.

Browner, C. H., Ortiz de Montellano, B. R., & Rubel, A. J. (1988). A methodology for cross-cultural ethnomedical research. *Current Anthropology, 29*, 681–702.

Buss, A. R., & Royce, J. R. (1975). Detecting cross-cultural commonalities and differences: Intergroup factor analysis. *Psychological Bulletin, 82*, 128–136.

Chon, K., Campbell, J. B., & Yoo, J. H. (1974). Extreme response style in cross-cultural research. *Journal of Cross-Cultural Psychology, 5*, 464.

Collett, P. (1972). Structure and content in cross-cultural studies of self esteem. *International Journal of Psychology, 7*, 169–179.

Dalal, A. (1984). Methodology of cross-cultural research: Some issues. *Indian Psychologist, 3*, 1–7.

Dalal, A. (1991). Idiographic research designs in cross-cultural psychology. *Indian Journal of Current Psychological Research, 6*, 61–71.

Drenth, P. J., & Van der Flier, H. (1976). Cultural differences and comparability of test scores. *International Review of Applied Psychology, 25*, 137–144.

Elequin, E. T. (1977). Organizing for cross-cultural research. *Topics in Culture Learning, 5*, 144–153.

Fegert, J. M. (1989). Bias factors in the translation of questionnaires and classification systems in international comparative child and adolescent psychiatric research. *European Journal of Child and Adolescent Psychiatry Acta Paedopsy, 52*, 279–286.

Gudykunst, W. B., & Kim, Y. Y. (1984). *Methods for intercultural communication research.* Newbury Park, CA: Sage.

Hanson, D. J. (1968). Equivalence in cross-cultural research. *Philippine Sociological Review, 16*, 51–60.

Harari, O., & Beaty, D. (1990). On the folly of relying solely on a questionnaire methodology in cross-cultural research. *Journal of Managerial Issues, 2*, 267–281.

Holtzman, W. H. (1979). Concepts and methods in the cross-cultural study of personality development. *Human Development, 22*, 281–295.

Hui, C. H., & Triandis, H. C. (1983). Multistrategy approach to cross-cultural research: The case of locus of control. *Journal of Cross-Cultural Psychology, 14*, 65–83.

Hui, C. H., & Triandis, H. (1985). Measurement in cross-cultural psychology: A review and comparison of strategies. *Journal of Cross-Cultural Psychology, 16*, 131–152.

Jaccard, J., & Wan, C. K. (1986). Cross-cultural methods for the study of behavioral decision making. *Journal of Cross-Cultural Psychology, 17*, 123–149.

Jian, U., & Misra, G. (1991). Reflections on psychology's scientific concerns. *Indian Journal of Current Psychological Research, 6*, 83–92.

Kleiner, R. J., & Barnallas, I. (1991). Advances in field theory: New approaches and methods in cross-cultural research. *Journal of Cross-Cultural Psychology, 22*, 509–524.

Kleiner, R. J., & Okeke, B. I. (1991). Advances in the field theory: New approaches and methods in cross-cultural research. *Journal of Cross-Cultural Psychology, 22*, 509–524.

Krause, M. S., & Howard, K. I. (1983). Design and analysis issues in the cross-cultural evaluation of psychotherapies. *Culture, Medicine and Psychiatry, 7*, 301–311.

Leigh, M. (1983). Ethnocentrism in cross-cultural research, and what to do about it. *Behavior Science Research, 18*, 213–227.

Leung, K., & Bond, M. H. (1989). On the empirical identification of dimensions for cross-cultural comparisions. *Journal of Cross-Cultural Psychology, 20,* 133–151.

Lipson, J. G., & Meleis, A. I. (1989). Methodological issues in research with immigrants. Special issue: Cross-cultural nursing: Anthropological approaches to nursing research. *Medical Anthropology, 12,* 103–115.

Lonner, W. J. (1986). Some methodological problems in cross-cultural media research. Special issue: Contributions to cross-cultural psychology. *Australian Journal of Psychology, 38,* 393–402.

Lonner, W., & Berry, J. (1986). *Field methods in cross-cultural research.* Newbury Park, CA: Sage.

Marin, G., & Marin, B. V. (1991). *Research with Hispanic populations.* Newbury Park, CA: Sage.

McDaniels, T. L. (1991). A framework for structuring cross-cultural research in risk and decision making. *Journal of Cross-Cultural Psychology, 22,* 141–149.

Meade, R. D., & Brislin, R. W. (1973). Controls in cross-cultural experimentation. *International Journal of Psychology, 8,* 231–238.

Mohanty, A., & Stewin, L. L. (1976). Cultural variables in conservation: A model for cross-cultural research. *Alberta Journal of Educational Research, 22,* 315–324.

Munson, J. M., & McIntyre, S. H. (1979). Developing practical procedures for the measurement of personal values in cross-cultural marketing. *Journal of Marketing Research, 16,* 48–52.

Ng, S. H. (1982). Choosing between the ranking and rating procedures for the comparison of values across cultures. *European Journal of Social Psychology, 12,* 169–172.

Pe-Pua, R. (1989). Pagtatanong-tanong: A cross cultural research method. *International Journal of Intercultural Relations, 13,* 147–163.

Sharma, S. (1977). Cross-cultural comparisons of anxiety: Methodological problems. *Topics in Culture Learning, 5,* 166–173.

Starr, B. J., & Wilson, S. F. (1977). Some epistemological and methodological issues in the design of cross-cultural research. *Topics in Culture Learning, 5,* 125–135.

Stole-Heiskanen, V. (1972). Contextual analysis and theory construction in cross-cultural family research. *Journal of Comparative Family Studies, 3,* 33–49.

Sutcliffe, C. R. (1974). Eliminating the biasing effects of social distance in cross-cultural survey research projects. *Journal of Social Psychology, 94,* 141–142.

Triandis, H., & Berry, J. (1980). *Handbook of cross-cultural psychology, vol. 2: Methodology.* Boston: Allyn & Bacon.

Triandis, H. C., & Brislin, R. W. (1984). Cross-cultural psychology. *American Psychologist, 39,* 1006–1016.

Triandis, H. C., Bontempo, R., Leung, K., & Hui, C. H. (1990). A method for determining cultural, demographic and personal constructs. *Journal of Cross-Cultural Psychology, 21,* 302–318.

Vega, W. A. (1992). Theoretical and pragmatic implications of cultural diversity for community research. *American Journal of Community Psychology, 20,* 375–391.

Vellerand, R. J. (1989). Vers une méthodologie de validation transculturelle de questionnaires psychologiques: Implications pour la recherche en langue française. (Toward a methodology for the transcultural validation of psychological questionnaires: Implications for research in the French language). *Canadian Psychology, 30,* 662–680.

Wagner, D. A., & Davis, D. A. (1978). The necessary and the sufficient in cross-cultural research. *American Psychologist, 33,* 857–858.